THE WRITER'S RIGHTS

Michael Legat

A & C Black · London

First published 1995
A & C Black (Publishers) Limited
35 Bedford Row, London WC1R 4JH

ISBN 0-7136-4018-9

A CIP catalogue record for this book is available
from the British Library.

The illustration on the front cover
is by Robin Hall.

Typeset by Janet Watson
Printed in Great Britain
by Biddles Ltd, Guildford, Surrey.

1001247291

THE
WRITER'S
RIGHTS

To Dominique

Also by Michael Legat

novels
Mario's Vineyard
The Silver Fountain
The Shapiro Diamond
The Silk Maker
The Cast Iron Man

non-fiction
Dear Author ...
An Author's Guide to Publishing
Writing for Pleasure and Profit
The Nuts and Bolts of Writing
Plotting the Novel
Non-fiction: an author's guide
How to Write Historical Novels
Understanding Publisher's Contracts
The Illustrated Dictionary of Western Literature
We Beheld His Glory
Putting on a Play

Contents

1
Freedom
of speech

Who are you writing for?

If you want to be a successful author, one of the most useful bits of advice that you could ever be given is to write first and foremost for your own pleasure. Write what you would like to read, and not what you think might tempt a publisher. Don't try to ape the latest fashion in bestsellers, unless that's really the kind of thing you enjoy reading and want to write. Most top-selling authors use this recipe. A perfect example of how it works can be seen in the famous Mills & Boon romances, which sell in enormous quantities worldwide. It comes as a surprise to many people to learn that they are one of the most demanding forms of fiction to write – and the main demand which they make is sincerity. You just can't write a Mills & Boon romantic novel unless you are sincere about it, unless you enjoy that kind of book yourself, unless you are happy writing it. Why is Dame Barbara Cartland so successful? Partly because she's very professional, and partly because she knows exactly the audience for whom she is writing – and number one in that audience is herself.

All this is not to say that you should disregard the market. If you want to be published, you will certainly have a better chance if you write something which is aimed specifically at a certain section of the reading public, and if you find out which publishers are most likely to be interested in your work. But the book still needs to be something that you believe in and really want to write.

The right to write

If you want to be published, it may be good advice to write only what you would yourself enjoy reading, but this does not mean that you have total freedom. If you write only for yourself, with no intention of publication, or even of letting anyone else see or hear your work, you can write anything at all, however libellous, however obscene, however blasphemous it may be, and you can plagiarise to your heart's content. You have an absolute right to write anything you like for your own exclusive, private use. Once you begin to aim at publication, however, you will come up against one or two restrictions.

The right to be published

It is perhaps worth pointing out, before looking at what those restrictions are, that however strong your right to write may be, you have no right at all to publication by a commercial publisher. Publishers can pick and choose, publish what they want to publish, and reject anything which does not appeal to them, whoever the author may be – and that is their undoubted right. If you are famous in some sphere or other, you will probably find it easier to get a book published than if you are unknown, but you still have to persuade a publisher to take your work on. In order to produce work which a publisher will believe is publishable, you must write something for which an editor will feel enthusiasm (or, at the very least, admiration for its professionalism). And it is also essential in almost every case that the publisher should believe that the book can be sold in sufficient quantities at a price which will enable a profit to be made on it (not all books by any means do make a profit, but that is the publisher's problem – the point is that the belief in the book's commercial potential must be there in the first place). Some books still manage to get published despite the fact that there is little chance of making money on them, either because the publisher feels that publication will substantially enhance the firm's reputation, or because a long-term view is taken in the hope that eventually future books from the same pen will bring in a good return on the initial investment. Alas, such cases are infrequent nowadays. Some years ago, the publisher Fredric Warburg, of the publishing firm Secker & Warburg, wrote an autobiography which he entitled ironically *An Occupation for Gentlemen*; publishing was probably never quite that even in his day, but it is certainly no longer anything of the sort (and I am not referring to the fact that women outnumber men in present-day publishing) – it is a cut-throat, commercial business.

There are occasional exceptions to the rules which I have been stating, and some books are published despite a total lack of enthusiasm from the publisher's editorial staff. These include those which are subsidised, either by a payment towards production costs – in the case of vanity publishing, usually a payment covering the entire costs of production and publication, plus the vanity publisher's profit - or a guarantee from the author or perhaps from a society or a business to buy a really substantial quantity of the book, often amounting to the entire edition. Subsidised publishing, except for the regrettable vanity houses, is comparatively rare. Of course, a bestselling author's books will almost certainly get published whether the editors like them or not, but at the start of his or her career that author needed an editor's enthusiasm to start the bandwaggon rolling.

Although a publisher has the right to accept or reject any book submitted, this does not mean that authors cannot write whatever they want (provided that it is legal), with some hope of publication. There are three or four hundred publishers in Britain – maybe even more – and between them they cover every conceivable kind of writing. And if, after trying every last one of them who might possibly be interested in taking your work on, you have had no luck, then, if you can afford it, there are always the vanity houses, or the much-to-be-preferred possibility of self-publishing (that is to say, arranging for your book to be printed, publishing it yourself and selling it yourself).

You may wonder, by the way, whether there is much difference between vanity publishing and self-publishing. Don't you have to be pretty vain as an author to use either method? Not necessarily. In any case, 'vanity publisher' is a technical term, used in the trade to refer to one of those concerns which will happily publish anything, however badly written, provided that the author is prepared to pay handsomely, not to say through the nose, for its services. They will print only a few copies of the book, there will be minimal sales, and although they will promise the author the most generous of royalties, the poor dupe will never see a single penny of his money back. You can always tell vanity publishers by their small ads in the papers, which use such phrases as 'Books Wanted!' or 'Looking for a Publisher?' In self-publishing, on the other hand, you pay for the manufacture of the book, but that is all, and you retain all the income that you generate from the sales. If you put a reasonable retail price on the book (something like three or four times the manufacturing cost), you can expect to recoup at least a part of your outgoings. Some self-publishing may be considered to be vain, but often it is simply a way of putting on the market a perfectly good book which has a limited sales appeal and therefore has not tempted any regular publisher. Self-publishing has become much more popular in recent years, especially since the sophisticated computers now available make 'desk-top publishing' possible (that is, the preparation of your material on your word processor, page by page, ready for printing). Whereas considerable opprobrium attaches to vanity publishing and you will lose a lot of money by it, self-publishing is quite respectable, and can even be profitable.

The writer and the law

The restrictions on your right to publish anything at all are largely based on the law of the land, rather than on an editor's preferences, although it is more than likely that a publisher would not be very keen on the kind of work which the law prohibits. If you self-publish a book you may not be affected by a publisher's editorial whims, but you are still going to be subject to the law. You can, of course, disregard it, and publish anyway, and you may even find a commercial firm which will be prepared to flout all the restrictions. After all, hard-core pornography gets into print. The problem is that if you are caught you may suffer a great deal.

But what does the law prohibit, and how clearly is the prohibited work defined? It is comparatively easy to itemise the kind of writing which may get you into trouble, but defining it is not always so simple. The difficult areas may be listed as: infringement of copyright, libel, obscene libel, blasphemous libel, sedition, and other offensive material (most of which has come to be what the devotees of political correctness are on about).

Infringement of copyright

Copyright is an important matter for any writer – a closer examination of it comes in Chapter 2 of this book.

To include in your book a substantial quotation from someone else's work without permission is an infringement of copyright, even if you give the source of the material, naming the author, the book and the publisher. What is worse is to copy someone's else's work without acknowledging the source, pretending that you have written it yourself. If you do that, you are guilty of plagiarism. Plagiarism, like piracy or unauthorised multiple photocopying, or any other infringement of copyright, is a crime, and a serious one. It is stealing, and there is no excuse for it.

Plagiarism can take four distinct forms. The first is a straight-forward, word for word reproduction of someone else's work which you incorporate into your own text. A variation on this is particularly applicable to fiction, and consists of leaving everything unchanged except for all the names of characters and places. (Whole novels have been plagiarised in this way. I remember particularly a story set in Korea at the time of the 1950s war there which was copied word for word except that the characters had been renamed and the whole action had been transferred to Italy during World War II. The publishers had accepted and published the book in all innocence, believing it to be an original work, but were nevertheless forced to pulp copies of the book and were heavily fined. Under the terms of their contract they undoubtedly had the right to claim compensation from the author, not only for the fine, but also for the pulped copies and the loss of profit on them, but whether they succeeded in getting him to repay any part of what he owed, I do not know.)

The second variety of plagiarism is the stealing of facts, which usually comes about through the author researching a subject by reading what other people have written, and then using the fruits of the research in his or her own work. It may seem difficult to avoid close similarities between your work and that of an earlier author – after all, if you are writing a book about, dahlias, say, or a biography of George V, there are certain facts, often forming a large proportion of your book, which will be common to all writings on the subject, and in presenting which the same terms will often demand to be used. Whether this sort of material has come out of your own existing knowledge of the subject or from research, there is usually little need to worry. Millions of facts are common knowledge and therefore common property, even if they happen not to be known to you personally. No charge of plagiarism can therefore be levelled if, for instance, you were to include in your own writing the name of various varieties of dahlia, or the date of the accession to the throne of King George V, even if you had had to look up such facts in someone else's book. The problem comes if you use a fact which is not generally known, which has been discovered by the author in whose book you found it, and which can be looked upon as that author's personal possession. If you acknowledge the provenance of the fact, and give the author credit for having ferreted it out, you will almost certainly be all right; if you use it without any indication that it is not all your own work, you are guilty of plagiarism. It is, of course, difficult sometimes to be certain of whether a given fact can be taken as generally known or not, but if you find only one source for it there is a distinct possibility that it is in copyright; the solution in any such case is, whenever in doubt, to say where you found it.

A third form of plagiarism is concerned with the general content of the book, or part of it. In any form of fiction, including drama, this usually means the plot. It is generally recognised that the number of basic plots is strictly limited – the rags to riches plot, the revenge plot, the love finds a way plot, and so on – and it may therefore seem impossible to avoid using a story line which has already provided the basis of a novel or short story or play for any number of authors. Does it matter? To authors who say that they can't think of a plot, the playwright David Campton says, 'Rewrite Cinderella

– practically every writer that I know has done so.' It is not, however, the basic plot, the theme, that we are talking about, but the approach of the author to that theme, the twists and turns which have been given to the basic plot. And if you follow too closely in the detailed plotting footsteps of another writer, you may well be guilty of plagiarism.

In non-fiction this form of plagiarism may be a matter of 'borrowing' whole arguments, ideas, themes from another book. Authors who want to use another author's material in this way are strongly advised not to do so. No doubt, by taking a lot of trouble you could make it appear that the work is all your own by so carefully paraphrasing it that you thereby disguise it. One of the ways in which this is sometimes done is by beginning with a direct quote from the copied work, for which permission is sought and paid for, but then going on to use all the original author's points in paraphrased form. Paraphrasing of any kind, without any acknowledgement of the original source, is never ethical, but undoubtedly some people write their books this way. However, so much skill is called for to make the copying invisible, not only by changing the words, but by making sure that the rhythms of the prose, the structure of the sentences and paragraphs, are not closely followed, that it would probably be easier to write one's own original material. It really is better to keep a clear conscience and be able to claim genuinely that what you produce is all your own work.

The fourth kind of plagiarism is concerned as much as anything with form, and is more often found in factual material rather than fiction. If, despite very careful paraphrasing, you keep too rigidly to the form of someone else's work, you may be in trouble. If, for instance, you were to write a book on an author's rights, and were to divide the subject up into exactly the same chapters as I have done, with similar sub-headings, and presentation of the various points in the same sort of order, I would certainly have a case against you, even if you had been very careful never to use my exact form of words.

What about unintentional plagiarism?

Supposing that you write something which turns out to be so like an already published book that you are accused of plagiarism. You have never seen the book which you are supposed to have copied, let alone read it, but how can you prove that? It's going to be very difficult to do so, especially if it is a work of fiction, because obviously you cannot be expected to have read even a fraction of the similar works published every year. So what defence can you make?

All you can do, probably, is to plead your innocence and find as many points of divergence as you can between the previously published work and your own.

One of the problems, whether you are concerned with fiction or non-fiction, is that you may have trouble with your subconscious. Almost everything you have ever read, and certainly anything which might have a bearing on your own work, is likely to be stored away in that remarkable part of the brain, ready to be trawled up at any time without any necessity for you to delve into it consciously. The subconscious is often fairly amoral, and will steal quite happily out of its store without your being aware of it at all. If you suspect that this may have happened, then you should re-read as much as possible of any books you have consulted in the course of your research, looking for anything which that naughty old subconscious might have copied.

In the case of non-fiction, if you are accused of plagiarism, you may be able to claim justifiably that any book on the subject is likely to make use of the same facts, and even to deal with them in the same order and with the same kind of comments. On the other hand, you will probably have read all the available books on the subject in the course of your research, so it would certainly be more difficult to make the case that you had no knowledge of work which you are said to have copied. However, during your research, you should be conscious of the need for your book to be different from the others (indeed, this may be a major selling point both when you are persuading a publisher to take it on and when the publisher wants to persuade members of the public to buy it).

If a work of fiction is concerned, the whole issue is likely to be much less clear-cut than with non-fiction, and similarities of plots or parts of plots can easily occur. Now, although you cannot read all the novels and short stories available, it is probably a good idea, if only for the sake of market research, to read the more popular writers producing work in your particular genre, and this should at least prevent you from coming up with a plot which is too similar to that used by Catherine Cookson, or Frederick Forsyth, or Iris Murdoch, or Martin Amis, or whoever is a leader in your field.

The plagiarised writer

Everything in this section so far has been warning you, the writer, against plagiarism. But of course you may be the offended party. If you suspect that your work has been copied, then don't hesitate to let your publisher know, and to take advice from him or her, and possibly also from the Society of Authors or the Writers' Guild if you are a member of either or both, about how to deal with the situation. You need to be sure of your case, and that means that the similarities between your own work and that of the offender are not merely of a coincidental nature, that they are not simply a rehearsing by both authors of generally-known facts, and that they are not so slight as to be hardly worth bothering about. But if you are sure, you should undoubtedly prosecute the offender without showing any mercy. Plagiarism is a criminal act.

Libel

Libel is a word which has always had the power to strike terror into a publisher's heart, and that power has been immensely increased in the last few years as a result of some highly publicised cases (not always involving books) in which enormous damages have been awarded to the plaintiffs. Apart from a few cynical and unscrupulous writers, mostly professionals, who are litigious by nature and who have realised that if you have no money to speak of, it doesn't much matter if you are ordered to pay vast damages, authors are often worried about the possibility of libelling someone in their work, and this is particularly true of would-be novelists, many of whom base their characters on people they know and are then terrified that a libel suit will ensue.

The first thing to understand is that libel is always written – the parallel word for the equivalent in speech is 'slander' (although broadcast material counts as libel). The second essential point is that you will not be guilty of libel unless you publish something about someone else which will harm that person's reputation in the eyes of anyone who might read what you have written, and who knows or can recognise the man or woman in question. By definition, libel is always damaging, or at least believed to be damaging, and is compounded if the harm is done not merely to the libelled person's reputation as a human being, but also to his or her professional or business standing. To write that your local butcher cheats at cards might well be libellous, but it would be libel of a far worse degree if you were to accuse him of selling contaminated meat. The fact that a statement about a person or a portrayal of a character is not libellous unless it is harmful means that you can put your friends and relations in your novel with impunity, as long as you do not present them in so unpleasant a light that they will feel damaged. You do not have to make them all squeaky-clean, saint-like people – they can have their little failings and foibles, and unless this kind of depiction will diminish them in the eyes of their friends and relations, you will have no trouble – at least, no legal trouble, although you may risk seriously upsetting those concerned. Putting someone into print, in however kindly a way, may be regarded as a breach of good manners, or, more offensively, as an invasion of privacy, and it could be very embarrassing for you if those who are aggrieved are close to you. This last point may particularly affect any portrait you paint in words of someone who is no longer living – you cannot libel the dead, but you can cause immense distress to relatives of the dead person by being too frank about his or her faults, as biographers often find. And while we are on the subject of libelling the dead, I should point out that, while neither the dead nor their descendants can normally sue you for libel, a suit could result if what you have said about the dead person has a direct and damaging bearing on the descendants.

What about disguising the character? Well, that depends on how effectively you can conceal the identity of the original on whom your 'fictional' character is based. It is certainly not enough to change the name. You will be well advised to change just about everything – age, appearance, circumstances, and even sex – and you may still find that if you have effectively captured the original's general behaviour and eccentricities, everyone will recognize him or her. Don't rely on the well-accepted 'fact' that when novelists put real people in their books, the originals never recognise themselves. It isn't true, and even if it were, there are always kind friends to tell the libelled person of what has been done to them.

There are also dangers to be encountered from strangers. If your novel has a character who is a professional person, such as a doctor or a lawyer, and who is also a criminal or extremely unpleasant, and if you happen to have chosen a name for this character which is that of a real-life practitioner in the field concerned, you could be sued, even though your character and all the circumstances surrounding him or her are entirely imaginary. A wise precaution is to check the lists of their members maintained by most professional bodies like the Law Society or the BMA to make sure that you use a name which does not appear in the list. There is in fact a defence against a libel suit, under the heading of 'innocence', if you have libelled someone accidentally, as you might in choosing by chance the name of a real-life person for a criminal or obnoxious character in your story. However, you would have to prove that you had no knowledge of the real-life person and no intention of referring to him or her, and that might be surprisingly difficult to do. In any case, it would involve you in quite a bit of expense, as any legal problems always do, so it is better to avoid trouble if you possibly can.

You can also find yourself in hot water if your novel has a villainous character who holds a position or an office which makes the real-life holder of that position or office a widely recognised public figure; so, for example, if you were to present the reader with a Chairman of a named major national industry who perhaps had his hand in the till or instigated a 'dirty-tricks' campaign against a competitor, you might be sued, even if you had invented a Chairman who was not in the least like the real-life person – the office itself being sufficient to identify him or her despite your attempts at disguise.

In non-fiction books, the problem is much simpler, because you can hardly libel someone accidentally, as in fiction, because you did not know of their existence, and you are not in any case forced into inventing a criminal or obnoxious character as you may be in the context of fiction. You must simply be aware that it is against the law to accuse anyone, even by implication, of anything which will be damaging to them, unless it is true. The perfect defence to a libel suit is that what you have written is the truth, the only problem being that the truth is often far more difficult to prove than you might think. You should not be tempted, unless it is quite unavoidable, to write anything deleterious if you can't prove it reasonably easily. The one exception to that rule is if you are merely repeating something which has been widely published previously and accepted as fact by everyone, including the libelled person, who has made no earlier attempt to sue. Even then, you need to be careful; if, for instance, you were to copy something, feeling safe because the libelled person had not brought an action against the original source of your harmful statement, it might simply be that for good reasons he or she had not got around to it yet, or that a subtle difference in your wording made your statement more objectionable than the original. Another example of possible danger is in writing about someone who has been convicted of a crime – which is a matter of record – but doing so in such a way that you damage the criminal, by suggesting perhaps that the person is not a reformed character. You have to be very careful, and in particular you should beware of allowing malice or anger on your own part to lead you into making harmful statements which you cannot support.

Two other defences against a libel suit exist. One, generally known as 'privilege', is usually confined to parliamentary reports and judicial statements, and therefore will not normally concern the ordinary writer. The other is 'fair comment', which protects journalists from trouble when, for instance, they accuse politicians and other public figures of incompetence and ignorance and of misleading and cheating the electorate, and which allows critics to write spiteful reviews. However, 'fair comment' does not necessarily similarly shield those whose accusations are concerned with the private life of these prominent people.

It is sometimes suggested that a solution to the possibility of being sued for libel is to show the text of your book to the person you are writing about in order to get clearance from them. It may be very helpful to have a written statement from the 'victim' to the effect that he or she has no objection to what you have written and even a guarantee that a libel suit will not be brought, but, alas, the person concerned may change his or her mind after publication, and would be entitled to do so if, for instance, the publicity given to what you have written brings the libellous matters into greater prominence.

You can, of course, always consult one of the lawyers who specialise in libel. Some publishers regularly submit books to such experts before putting them into print. It's an expensive business, but well worth it if a court case can be avoided as a result of the advice received. There is still a risk, however, for even the most experienced of libel lawyers can pass as innocuous some obscure statement which later results in the author and the publisher having to pay large-scale damages.

Obscene Libel

Obscene Libel is the legal term for the production and publication of pornography and other offensive material, such as descriptions of excessive violence, which, in the terms of the old definition, has 'a tendency to deprave and corrupt' those who read it. You probably think that in the present climate of opinion it is hardly worth mentioning obscene libel as an offence for perpetrating which the author might fear prosecution; society seems to have decided that, while a few Puritans may tut-tut their disapproval, anyone who wants to do so may freely write, publish or buy hardcore pornography without much of a let or hindrance, since no one except those who are already depraved and corrupted is likely to be harmed by it. In every major city in every fully 'developed' country of the world (which leaves out China and a few Islamic countries) it is easy to find a hundred shops selling material which fifty years ago would have been considered highly offensive.

However, despite this freedom, in most civilised countries there are still laws which prohibit the production of pornographic works, and although the authorities mostly pretend that such laws do not exist, there is a limit to their tolerance. A difference exists between pornography and what might be termed acceptable descriptions of sexual acts, although the dividing line is a very thin one, and any current bestseller list can be guaranteed to contain novels which a generation ago would have been considered obscene. It is extremely difficult to define that difference, which is perhaps why it has been necessary to add 'hardcore' to 'pornography' to distinguish the totally explicit material which is produced solely with the intention of titillating or sexually stimulating the reader or watcher. So, let us forget 'pornography' and concentrate on 'hardcore pornography'.

From time to time the British police or officials of the Customs & Excise seize obscene material, and although they sometimes make fools of themselves by including perfectly respectable books in their haul, misled perhaps by the title, their actions are generally applauded by the public at large. For the most part, the books and magazines seized will be destroyed, and the bookseller will appear in a magistrate's court to be fined, but nothing much beyond that is likely to happen. However, society can still be very censorious about hardcore pornography which caters for the rather more exotic sexual tastes, such as sadism, bondage and especially paedophilia, and a major prosecution is always on the cards for those who produce and market it. While there is nothing to stop you from writing seriously and sensitively on such taboo subjects, if hardcore pornography of that kind is your own bag, by all means write it for your private pleasure, and publish it if you must, but don't expect any sympathy if you get caught and severely punished (except, I suppose, from your fellow sadists, bondage fetishists and paedophiles).

Four-letter words

In times gone by, the use of the so-called 'four-letter words' might have resulted in a prosecution for obscene libel. Even as late as the 1960s few respectable publishers would allow an author to use such shocking words, and the celebrated *Lady Chatterley's Lover* case (which largely brought about the end of an era of censorship) was not only concerned with the description of the sexual act which the novel contained, but the horrifying words used to describe it. Among the conservative middle classes, even so mild a word as 'bloody' was not used in the presence of a female – at least, not without an apology - although the four-letter words were widely known and used in circumstances, such as the rugger club bath, where no one would be offended by them. Nowadays, a novel which does not contain the 'f- word' is a rarity, and that and other 'obscenities', as they used to be called, are scattered through the text of some books with the utmost liberality. Anything goes, and as a writer you are unlikely to encounter any trouble because of your 'bad' language. The one reservation which can be made on this score, however, is a matter of style and effective writing rather than a legal problem, and that is that 'strong' words can often have a dramatic effect, but not if they are used too frequently. Shaw knew exactly what he was doing in the tea-party scene in *Pygmalion*; had he been entirely truthful in his portrait of Eliza Doolittle she would undoubtedly have been using a variety of swear words throughout her conversation, but the effect was made devastating by the use of the single 'bloody' (shocking in 1916, especially spoken by a woman at a ladies' tea-party). So use 'four-letter words' if you want to, but use them to good effect. And the same applies, of course, to the scenes of detailed and specific sex and/or violence which you put into your novel – the more frequent such scenes, the less their impact will become.

Blasphemous Libel

The law still prohibits blasphemy, which it calls Blasphemous Libel, and by which it means writing or saying anything which is irreverent, or demeaning, or even exceptionally critical about the principal figures in the Christian religion and about Christianity in general (but, in practice, at least in most of Britain, probably only the Anglican version). However, you would almost certainly have to produce something exceptionally offensive in that line to run much risk of prosecution nowadays. We are almost completely unshockable. The majority of the population, having at best a nominal interest in religion, doesn't care, and even the practising Christian is likely to shrug off blasphemy as unfortunate, but not to be taken seriously. A bishop or two might protest, but that is about all that would happen, and it would soon be forgotten.

But it's not the same when it comes to other religions, as Mr Salman Rushdie well knows, and although you cannot be prosecuted in this country for blasphemy in respect of Islam or Judaism or Hinduism or any other non-Christian religion, you can be condemned to death without trial by people who do not live in Britain, but who can find plenty of residents in this country and throughout the world who would be happy to carry out the sentence if they had the opportunity. So you are in fact in much greater danger in Britain if you blaspheme against a religion which is neither the official religion of the country nor protected by law than if you attack Christianity, even if it's the Anglican variety. And because some of the non-Christian religious groups in Britain are militant and vociferous, it is quite likely that one day their pleas will be heard and our blasphemy laws will be altered so as to cover all religions. If that happens, there is no reason to suppose that the non-Christian sects will be as tolerant as Christians – they will be easily offended, and swift in retribution.

Since religion is so personal a matter, you must follow your own conscience in writing about it, but, as with everything in this chapter, you must be circumspect and avoid giving offence if you possibly can.

Sedition

It is hard to imagine that any author in Britain would be prosecuted for trying to bring down the monarchy or even for an attempt at putting an end to Parliament – at least, not if the 'sedition' were confined to anti-monarchist or anti-democratic writings, although, of course, you can still be tried for an attempt on the Queen's life, or for trying to blow up Parliament. But what is far more at risk than either Her Majesty or the Houses of Commons and Lords is the security of the state, and for endangering the state you could easily find yourself with a long jail sentence. You are in fact unlikely to be in that sort of position unless you are in possession of secret information of one kind or another. Governments always want to keep certain things secret (Oppositions, of course, always want all information to be freely available), and place restrictions on those who work for them, so that civil servants, members of the armed services and various other people in government employment are not supposed to publish their memoirs or accounts of past events in which they have been involved without having their work officially approved before publication, even if no state secrets are concerned. However, a respected ex-Ambassador recently got away with it, although his revelations were indiscreet rather than seditious. A more relevant case was the great hoo-ha a few years back over a rather dreary book called *Spycatcher*, which offended against government restrictions. If you are contemplating a book which might breach the Official Secrets Act, you will have to weigh up the likelihood of a successful prosecution, which might be very unpleasant (unless you are sensible enough, like the author of *Spycatcher*, to have removed yourself beforehand to Australia or somewhere equally remote), against the chance of enormous sales.

Other offensive material

The current vogue for political correctness comes to us from across the Atlantic. That is not to say that no fanatical devotees of p.c. exist in Britain, but the inspiration was certainly generated in the United States and was an expansion of such ideas as anti-racism and of feminism. Political correctness consists in fact of saying or writing nothing which could be offensive to anyone else, and it covers all conceivable -isms, from racism and sexism through to classism, ageism, heightism, weightism, disabilityism, etc., etc..

Most people would agree that language which is offensive to certain sections of the human race should be avoided. The trouble is that the gurus of political correctness sometimes go overboard, especially if they are particularly concerned to ensure that a certain -ism is observed; so the extreme feminists made fools of themselves by insisting on 'ploughperson's lunch' and 'personholes' in the street, and there were even suggestions of renaming that great northern city as Personchester (although that example was undoubtedly no more than a malicious joke on the part of someone who was opposed to what was being done to the language by the more militant feminists).

Once political correctness began to take hold, there was no stopping it. Employees everywhere apparently discovered, quite suddenly, that they were demeaned by their job description, or by the way that people referred to their distinguishing qualities. So a dustman had to become at least a 'refuse collector' if not a 'hygiene operative' and someone who was lame might be described as 'mobility–disadvantaged'. It never seems to bother those who preach the necessity of political correctness that many people who care for language are very much distressed by the ignominy which has been attached by p.c. to many entirely respectable and useful words of ancient lineage.

One of the problems with politically correct terminology is that in some cases it is rather more insulting than the words it replaces, and another is that it is sometimes difficult to know which particular epithet is currently in favour – no one could seriously dispute the need to stop the common usage of the highly offensive word 'nigger' (offensive because it was always used by white people with a sense of contempt – c.f. the equally nasty 'wog', 'Jew-boy', 'slit-eye', etc.), but for a time one had to substitute 'Negro', and then 'Negro' became a forbidden word and was replaced by 'black', which is still widely acceptable, except that there is some insistence nowadays on the use of a word denoting nationality with the prefix 'Afro-', to give 'Afro-American' or 'Afro-Caribbean' or even 'Afro-English' – all very confusing.

How much notice do you have to take of political correctness? The only one of the -isms which is actually prohibited by law as far as written work is concerned is racism, which consists of derogatory comments or attacks on ethnic groups. 'Ethnic', by the way, derives from the Greek word for 'nation', but its primary

English dictionary meaning is specifically 'not belonging to the Christian or Jewish religion'; of course it is used nowadays to refer to any minority or oppressed group and especially to those people whose skin is not white. However, although racism may be the only prosecutable offence, a writer will be wise to try to avoid objectionable words which might upset any of his or her potential readers, including the editors who will decide whether or not to publish the work. Among other things, that will probably mean using the clumsy 'he or she' or 'his or her' where a simple 'he' or 'his' would have been acceptable in the past (there are ways of getting round the problem – by using the plural, for instance – but it is not always practical to do so).

The most difficult problems arise in writing for children. Publishers, librarians, booksellers and teachers, and even some of the adults who buy books for children are acutely aware of the need to avoid anything which will fail to reflect the modern multicultural world in which none of the stereotypes of the past can be taken for granted. For instance, two-parent families in which the father is the sole breadwinner are perceived to be not quite so normal and standard as they used to be, and although they may still be very much in the majority, a writer for children will possibly have a better chance of success if writing about a different domestic situation of some kind; as for train sets for boys and dolls for girls, such ideas are quite suspect. If you are interested in writing for children, you will have very little hope of publication if you ignore the taboos.

2
Copyright

What is copyright?

Although we think of 'copyright' as meaning something rather similar to 'ownership', the term began life (in 1757, says *The Shorter Oxford English Dictionary*) simply as an amalgam of the two words 'copy' and 'right' and meant, literally, 'the right to copy'. In fact, that basic meaning remains valid, but because of the way we use the word, not to mention the developments since the eighteenth century in the way that creative work is made available to the public at large, we need to expand our definition. My edition of *The Shorter OED* states that copyright is 'the exclusive right given by law for a certain term of years to an author, composer, etc. (or his assignee) to print, publish, and sell copies of his original work'. Even that, however, seems to me to be incomplete without the additional wording, 'or to license others to do so', since, despite the rise in self-publishing, it is still the exception rather than the rule for the creative person – the author, composer, artist, photographer, et al. – to be the one to 'print, publish, and sell copies of his original work'. One cannot quarrel, on the other hand, with the additional definitions of 'copyright' as an adjective, meaning 'protected by copyright' (e.g. a copyright article), and as a transitive verb, meaning 'to secure copyright for' (e.g. to copyright an article).

Leaving dictionary definitions on one side, the subject of copyright, as it affects authors, both published and unpublished, in practical terms, can be immensely complex. Whole books are written about it, lawyers wrangle over it, and, like most aspects of the law, it can prove an impenetrable jungle for the legally untutored writer who gets in trouble over it. Fortunately, however, most authors will find that, while copyright is of prime importance to them, for practical purposes they will need little more than a basic knowledge of the subject.

For a start, it can be said, in simple terms, that as far as authors are concerned, copyright means effectively that anything original that any person writes, whether for publication or not, is automatically copyright as soon as it is written, whether the words appear on paper or on a word processor disc or on a tape recorder or in any other tangible form, without necessarily being published; and it is protected by law, both in Britain and in almost all other countries of the world, against unauthorised use by any other person or organisation. This does not apply only to literary works, but to letters, notices and any other original writings. 'Original' in this context does not mean that the work must be innovative, unusual or even literate, let alone literary, but that it has not been copied from anyone else's work, and that the author has worked, however minimally, to produce it. The copyright in your shopping list belongs to you. But, please note, that whatever it may be, the material is copyright only if it has been written down or recorded in some way. A speech is not copyright, unless the orator has put it in writing or recorded it on tape or disc.

The ownership of the copyright lies with the originator of the work, or jointly if there is more than one originator, although it can, of course, be assigned as a whole or in part to another person or persons, or to a business concern such as a publisher (although it is preferable, as will be explained later, to *license* the use of the material to a second party, rather than to assign the copyright). An assignment, which means giving up your copyright, must be in writing and signed by or on behalf of the assignor, whereas a licence, which means that you retain the copyright but allow other parties to exploit certain aspects of your work, need not be in writing; an oral licensing agreement may therefore be valid, and in some cases no agreement at all is necessary, as with a letter sent for publication to a newspaper.

The main exception to this rule of author-ownership is that it does not apply to material written for an employer as part of the author's normal employment by that employer (especially when there is a contract of employment between them), unless the employer and employee have specifically agreed otherwise. So the copyright in a private letter belongs to its writer, while a business letter is the copyright of the employer (although in either case the ownership of the letter itself, as an artefact, lies with the recipient). In the same way, as we shall see later, the work of journalists is their own copyright if they are working on a freelance basis, but will almost certainly belong to the owners of the newspaper or magazine if they are staff writers employed by the newspaper or magazine in question. This unfortunately applies nowadays even if the employee reworks the basic material into a different form.

One further case where copyright exists is in the typographical arrangements of published editions. This is a copyright normally owned by the publisher of the work, and it means, for example, that when the rights in a work have reverted, the author is entitled to republish it without let or hindrance, but must not photograph or otherwise reproduce the type of the original edition without the publisher's permission.

A brief history of copyright

In his book, *Authors and Owners: the Invention of Copyright*, Professor Mark Rose explains that the first British legislation to state categorically that authors had any rights of ownership over their works came with the so-called Act of Anne, which was passed in 1710, predating the first appearance of the word 'copyright' itself. Before that time authors had, of course, been paid for their work – the example of Milton selling what we should now call 'the copyright' in *Paradise Lost* for ten pounds (and a further ten pounds if it sold well enough, which it didn't) is well known – and those early authors might even have been able to take legal action against any unauthorised person producing and selling copies of what they had written, but the 1710 Act was the first true enshrinement of the principle of copyright within the law of the land.

It was, however, a somewhat rudimentary statement of the author's rights, and it was not until the nineteenth century that any real similarities to today's British copyright laws began to emerge, in particular with a definition of the period of time for which copyright would last. In 1842 a law was passed giving authors copyright in their works for their lifetime and seven years after their death, or for a minimum of forty-two years after publication. A further advance came with the Copyright Act of 1911, which increased the copyright period to the author's lifetime plus fifty years after death, or fifty years after posthumous publication, and this term of copyright remained in force in the Copyright Act of 1956.

Then came the 1988 Copyright, Designs and Patents Act. This did not alter the fifty-year period either, except in respect of posthumously published works, in which the fifty years of copyright begin from the date of the author's death, rather than from publication, unless the author's identity is unknown. Incidentally, the fifty-year period always starts from the end of the year in which the author dies, and in the case of joint authorship is taken from the year when the last of the collaborating authors dies. During the fifty year period, the copyright belongs to the author's estate.

The 1988 Act clarified a number of previously contentious issues, made other matters pretty incomprehensible to most ordinary people (and, one suspects, to lawyers, too), and introduced some new concepts, such as Moral Rights (see p.33). It also included some useful definitions, among which are an explanation of the kind of property in which copyright can exist (original literary, dramatic, musical or artistic works, sound recordings, films, and broadcasts or cable programmes) and a ruling on the meaning of 'literary work' (any work, other than a dramatic or musical work, which is written, spoken or sung, including a table or compilation, a computer program and preparatory design material for a computer program).

A further change to our copyright laws is about to come into force. It will not surprise any British reader to learn that copyright has attracted the interest of the bureaucrats in Brussels – it is a tailor-made subject for them – but authors and other creative artists will be happy to discover that in this case the European Union's 'harmonisation' is working in their favour. The directive is that as from July 1st 1995, the period of copyright shall be extended to seventy years after death. At the time of writing, it is not clear when a new British Act will be drafted and eventually passed, nor exactly what provisions it will include, nor how existing works will be affected. Will books which have recently gone out of copyright be brought back into copyright? Will publishers whose contracts give them a licence for 'the full legal term of copyright' get an additional twenty years automatically? What will happen to posthumous works and works by authors who live outside the European Union (which includes, of course, many English-speaking countries)? These and many other difficult problems will have to be solved. A further complication is that books which are in copyright in any one of the member states of the EU will be considered to be in copyright in all the other member states, regardless of any local laws, which presumably means that a work which is out of copyright in any of the member states will have to be drawn back into copyright in those states if in just one other state its copyright is still valid.

It may be a long time before all the complex problems are sorted out and the harmonisation process is complete. Generally speaking, however, the outlook is for an improved copyright position for authors and their inheritors – eventually.

As a rule, whenever new copyright acts are introduced provision is made for works published prior to the new act to continue to be protected by the act which was in force at the time of publication. So, to take the example already mentioned of the difference between the 1988 Act and its 1956 predecessor, books which were published posthumously before 1st August 1989 still enjoy full copyright for fifty years from the date of publication, rather than from the date of the author's death. Similarly, whatever changes are made as a result of the EU directive, the 1988 Act will continue to protect those books which do not fall within the provisions of any new legislation.

The Berne Convention

The European Union is not the only foreign influence on Britain's copyright laws. We have been involved in the framing of international copyright agreements, and affected by them, for well over a hundred and fifty years. In 1886, as a result of conferences held in Berne, Switzerland, a number of countries signed an agreement known as the Berne Convention, which guaranteed authors the same protection for their works in signatory countries as the natives of those countries enjoyed. No formalities were required, and both published and unpublished works were fully covered as soon as they were written down on paper or any other suitable material. Over the years, the Berne Convention has been revised many times, and the number of signatories subscribing to it has increased from the original nine (the British Empire, Belgium, France, Germany, Italy, Spain, Switzerland and – how extraordinary, given the way the world worked at that time – Tunis and Haiti) to over sixty. For many years the most notable absentees from the list of signatories were the United States of America (unable to join because of its own copyright laws, which insisted on local manufacture before copyright protection could be given), the Soviet bloc, and China.

The Universal Copyright Convention

The Berne Convention has been largely superseded in the public mind (insofar as the public is aware of copyright at all) by the Universal Copyright Convention, although Berne is still in effect and exists, as it were, in parallel with the UCC. The latter originated in 1952 under the auspices of UNESCO. Ratified by the United Kingdom in 1957, it is widely recognised throughout the world, and both the United States and Russia eventually became signatories. Not unexpectedly China has remained out of step, although welcome signs of greater respect for international copyright have recently appeared there. You may think that the fact that the convention can justifiably call itself 'Universal' is a matter for rejoicing, and so it is; however, the UCC is not quite as generous as it might be, since its minimum term of copyright is the lifetime of the author and only twenty-five years after death, or, in some countries, no more than twenty-five years from first publication. Fortunately, the majority of signatories, while observing the UCC, still work under the Berne Convention and their own domestic laws and offer both native and foreign authors the more acceptable lifetime plus fifty (or, even better, seventy) years after death as the term of copyright.

It was the UCC which introduced the familiar symbol © , which, followed by the author's name and the date of publication, must appear on the work in question if it is to be accepted as copyright in the signatory countries. Since the symbol © means 'copyright' it is unnecessary – indeed, tautological – to precede the symbol with the word 'Copyright', as is often done. Originally, it was insisted that the copyright line should show the author's real name in full, including all first names as well as the surname, which resulted in the revelation of the true identity of a number of writers previously known only by their pseudonyms. Nowadays, however, copyright is usually registered in the name of the author as it appears on the title page, whether or not it is pseudonymous or incomplete, unless the copyright has been assigned to someone else or to a company (many authors – mostly the more successful ones – find that it pays them for tax purposes to turn themselves into limited liability companies which then become the proprietors of their copyrights).

The USA, which for decades had lagged behind the rest of the developed countries as far as copyright for non-nationals was concerned, finally took the plunge, rescinded its insistence that copyright protection should not be fully granted unless the work had been printed in the United States, and joined the Universal Copyright Convention in 1955. Even then, it limited the initial, automatic copyright period to twenty-eight years (renewal was possible), and insisted that any work which did not carry the standard copyright line (e.g. *Copyright* © *A.N. Other* [copyright owner's name] *19—*, although either the symbol © or the word 'Copyright' could be omitted) should be regarded as in the public domain and could therefore be printed and published without the permission of the author and without payment of any royalties or fees. Happily, the United States later went farther, and brought in a new copyright law which enabled it in 1989 to become a signatory of the Berne Convention. British authors therefore now enjoy the same protection in the United States as their American cousins, including the continuation of copyright for fifty years after death. However, for books copyrighted in the States prior to 1978 it is necessary to apply in the twenty-eighth year after the copyright was first taken out for a renewal period of a further forty-seven years, making a total of seventy-five years regardless of when the author dies. Although, in order to secure copyright in the States, it is no longer essential for an author who is not an American citizen to register a work first published outside the United States by depositing a copy with the Library of Congress, it is certainly still vital to ensure that it bears a copyright notice, either using the symbol © or the word 'Copyright'.

When to surrender your copyright

Your copyright is, or should be, of supreme importance to you. It may be very valuable in financial terms, but even if you do not expect to make any money from what you have written, you should never, as a matter of principle, part with your copyright. Never? Well, hardly ever – there are a few exceptional circumstances, and we shall look at these later. But the principle of 'no surrender' remains valid in almost all cases. Of course, you may wish to hand over your copyright to a relative or friend, but even if you are thinking on these lines it may be preferable to assign all income from the work to the person concerned, but still to keep your copyright.

Most book publishers will respect the author's wish to retain copyright, but some will demand its surrender; if the author protests, the answer may be that the sum offered as the purchase price of the copyright (often referred to as an 'outright' payment) is generous, that the publisher always works that way (with the misleading implication that the author is the one who is out of step with normal trade practice), and, if the author continues to protest, that there are plenty of other good fish in the sea (a form of blackmail which is even more frequently to be found in the world of journals and magazines – see Chapter 10); the contract may then be lost to another writer who is tempted by the ready cash on offer and does not see the dangers in surrendering copyright. Those dangers are not only the possible loss of royalties, which could involve enormous sums if the book turns into a steady bestseller, plus moneys from subsidiary rights, including translations and publication in the United States, but also the possibility that the work could be altered in any way that the new copyright owner thought fit – possibly mutilated to such an extent that the original author might consider it damaging both personally and professionally – and yet that author would have no recourse against the publisher. It is easy, of course, to adopt a moralising attitude and to condemn those authors who agree to sell their copyright, without understanding that the temptation of a comparatively large sum of money offered as an outright payment may be irresistible to a writer in financial difficulties, or to one who is so eager to get into print that the terms seem unimportant. Nevertheless, all authors, as a matter of principle, and because to surrender one's copyright in this way is to betray one's fellow-writers, should refuse any such publishing offers.

I have been writing so far about the copyright in an individual full-length book of a general nature. A publisher will occasionally make out a case for the author's surrender of copyright if the book is part of a series, especially if it has been written at the publisher's request and to his or her very detailed specifications. The argument is that the publisher needs copyright control of all the books in the series, because as a series it might in some ways be regarded as a single title. Well, up to a point, Lord Copper. I still think that any sensible author should fight vigorously to retain copyright, while giving the publisher as much freedom as possible when licensing the rights to him or her, and undertaking not to be obstructive in respect of the publisher's negotiations for the series as a whole.

Publishers have rather more justification for asking to control the copyright in the case of encyclopaedias and other books to which a large number of authors contribute. The publishers of such books usually insist that copyright in the articles included should be vested in them, again pleading the necessity to have total control, especially in the event of piracy or other infringements. It may be a more legitimate case, but even so, it should not be beyond the wit of the contracts department of such publishers to draw up a document which gives the company the required freedom and still allows the author to retain copyright.

One danger in respect of unpublished work occasionally lurks in the rules of the short story competitions which proliferate nowadays. Apart from the usual provisions that entries should not have been published, and sometimes should not have been entered for any other competition, the rules often give the organisers of the competition the right to publish the work of the prizewinners, and possibly also that of the runners-up. This is fair enough – you will probably welcome the idea of seeing your work in print, and some cash reward is usually paid. You should make sure, however, that you do not, by signing the entry form, give the organisers the copyright in your work, or even unlimited use of the story. All that you should offer them is First British Serial Rights, or possibly First European Serial Rights (see Chapter 10).

Although 'never' should be the watchword as far as the surrender of copyright is concerned, there may be occasions, as has already been suggested, when 'hardly ever' might be more appropriate. All the circumstances surrounding the purchase of the work have to be taken into consideration, but if, as a result, you absolutely must surrender your copyright, don't do so without arguing first, and making it plain that you think the very idea is iniquitous, even if you have to do so politely for fear of upsetting the publisher and perhaps losing the commission (which you probably won't). And do make sure that you get a large enough sum to compensate, at least to as great an extent as possible, for your potential loss of future earnings and control of your work.

How to protect your copyright

As explained above, under the Universal Copyright Convention it is necessary to include in any published work a copyright line, which normally consists of the word 'Copyright', followed by the copyright symbol © , the name of the author(s) (usually as shown on the title page) or copyright owner and the date of first publication. Most book publishers will include this line without any prompting from the author (it is in their interest to make sure that anyone looking at the book will know that it is fully protected against unauthorised use, even if they do not themselves own the copyright). In any case, their contracts usually include a clause stating not only that they will ensure that such a notice appears in all copies of the work which they publish, but that they will pass on a similar obligation to any other sub-contractor, such as a paperback publisher, bookclub, or foreign publisher, to whom they grant a licence to produce the book in some other form.

Supposing that your work is published without any copyright notice – have you lost your copyright? Not unless you have assigned it to any other person or company. The Copyright, Designs and Patents Act of 1988 makes no mention of a copyright notice as a requirement before copyright can be recognised. Your work is copyright simply because you have written it. So why is there all this fuss about copyright notices, and are they really important? Although the copyright notice is not essential in Britain, and by extension in all countries which are signatories of the Berne Convention, it is still a requirement under the Universal Copyright Convention. But even within the Berne Convention countries the printing of the copyright notice warns off anyone who, unaware that the work is still protected, might think of making unauthorised use of the material if the notice were not there.

What about unpublished work? Do you need to put a copyright line on your typescript? Well, it won't do any harm, and you could, if you like, include a copyright page, bearing a standard copyright notice, in the 'prelims' (the preliminary pages – title page, list of contents, etc.) of your typescript, putting the date of the year in which you are submitting the book to a publisher. However, it is really not necessary to do this, at least for all countries which are signatories of the Berne Convention, in which all work is protected without any formalities being required. If, on the other hand, you are going to send your work to the USA, it is probably a good idea to add such a notice.

But is that really sufficient, either in Britain or abroad? Many authors, and especially perhaps those who have not yet succeeded in breaking into print, worry that unscrupulous publishers will return their typescripts with a rejection slip, but only after copying them so that they can steal the work and publish it, possibly with a few minor cosmetic changes, under some other author's name. How can you guard against becoming the victim of such criminal behaviour?

From time to time companies are set up with the professed purpose of protecting the copyright of unpublished works, registering them on a database after the author has submitted a copy of the work in the appropriate form (typescript, tape, CD-ROM, etc.), plus, of course, a fee. The fee is usually something in the order of £25 per work, in addition to a substantial annual membership subscription. Have nothing to do with any organisation offering copyright protection, however impressive their brochure may be. You will not gain anything more than you could by mailing yourself a sealed copy of the work, keeping the parcel unopened, with the date stamp to prove when it was written, or by placing a sealed copy in a bank, with a dated receipt. The brochures of copyright protection organisations often sneer at such primitive procedures – naturally they want to persuade you to use their expensive services. I am myself tempted to sneer a little, or at least not to recommend these more modest practices, although I know that some tutors of Creative Writing tell their students firmly that they should follow them. In over fifty years in the book business I have never met a professional author who feels it necessary to bother with a performance of this kind. Reputable publishers don't steal authors' work – quite apart from the fact that most of them are honest, upright citizens, it simply doesn't pay them to behave so unscrupulously and thereby damage their reputations. 'Ah, but not all publishers are reputable,' you may say. True, but you will be extremely unlucky if you come across one of the real rogues. And if you do believe that a publisher has stolen your work, then you have a remedy in the law of copyright, and can bring a legal action against the thief.

But do make sure that you have a sound basis for your accusations before you launch into them. In the case of fiction, if your complex and unusual plot seems to have been copied in complete detail, or almost exactly, you probably have a legitimate grievance and could bring a successful suit for infringement of your copyright (provided, of course, that you can prove the originality of your own work and that the offending parties had the opportunity of copying it). However, bearing in mind that it is extremely difficult to be original in plotting, it must be said that similarity of plot is usually little more than coincidence. You need to be sure that the infringement (if it is that) goes beyond anything which a judge could consider to be coincidental.

In non-fiction, the points of comparison may be largely a matter of repeating known facts and widely-shared attitudes towards them (although finding in someone else's book a fact which you could prove was previously known only to you as a result of your own private researches might well be cause for a suit – see p. 5). Of course, if you see that your own idiosyncratic arrangement of the facts has been followed exactly, that all the original ideas appear in the book in the same order, then you may be justified in pursuing the matter. But again, make absolutely sure that the apparent copying could not possibly be a mere coincidence.

Bear in mind that if you bring a case of this kind you are quite likely to be faced by a plagiarist who will brazenly deny ever having seen your book and insist that the work you complain of is entirely original. And ranged against you will be a team of lawyers skilled in denigrating your claim and in proving their client's innocence. It is not always easy to prove plagiarism has taken place, so you need to be certain of what you say.

If you do have a case of this nature, it will obviously be strength-ened if the wording is exactly the same in both your version and the offending one, and indeed this may be the strongest proof of all that the work has been copied. But the similarities do need to be extensive – the odd sentence, or perhaps a line of dialogue in fiction, will not provide sufficient evidence.

Naturally, if you meet a nasty situation of this kind, it will be a great help if you can substantiate your claim with details of when your book was written, when it was submitted to the publisher in question, and so on. You will, of course, when submitting your work, send it with a covering letter, and, unless you receive no more than an undated rejection slip, you will have a letter from the publisher when your material comes back to you. Keep copies of any correspondence – keep the wrapper that the publishers used to send your book back, if you want to. It may all be useful if you have to bring a lawsuit because your copyright has been infringed. But let me repeat that generally speaking you don't need to have sleepless nights – the villains who will snaffle your work exist almost entirely only in your imagination.

Copyright after death

As has already been stated, copyright endures for fifty (soon to be seventy) years after the author's death, and is part of his or her estate. The ownership of the copyright in the author's work or works depends, however, on what provisions if any have been made for their disposal in a Will. Copyrights can be of considerable value to legatees, and this applies not only to published works, but to unpublished ones too. The wise author will therefore make careful disposal of these rights, leaving them perhaps to one heir or, if many works exist, splitting them among a number of beneficiaries. Some authors generously leave their copyrights, or some of them, to a charity – the Royal Literary Fund or the Authors' Foundation would be particularly apt. If no special provision is made, any copyrights will simply form part of the estate and will pass to the residual legatee.

A problem may exist for legatees who become the owners of various copyrights under the author's Will if they have no experience of publishing and no knowledge of how to exploit the rights they have been given. An agent, if the author had one, will probably be willing to act on behalf of the person who has inherited the property. If the author did not have an agent, it may be possible to persuade one to handle the posthumous work, but probably only if that work is substantial and is likely to bring in a reasonable income. If that is not the case, the legatee may be able to find someone, perhaps among the dead author's professional friends, who would be willing to act as 'literary executor', a term which has no legal standing, but which is used generally for a person looking after a literary estate on behalf of legatees who, for whatever reason, are incapable of handling the matter themselves, or are unwilling to do so.

One of the problems which a legatee or a literary executor may face is the valuation of the deceased author's copyrights, which the Capital Taxes Office may require. Help can usually be obtained from the author's publisher or agent.

Piracy

By the term 'piracy' the book trade means the publishing of unauthorised editions, without payment of any fees, of works which have previously been issued in the normal way by a publisher who has the right to do so. It is a matter of grave concern to authors and publishers the world over - a pirated edition can, in the country where it is produced, bring sales of the original, authorised edition to a standstill. English-language publishers and writers are particularly affected because English is so widely spoken, although it has to be admitted that the problem relates only to books, mostly international bestsellers and educational titles, which will find a ready market in the country where the pirate publisher operates.

A hundred years or so ago, the greatest danger of piracy for British writers and publishers lay across the Atlantic. Anyone who knows the history of the Gilbert and Sullivan operettas will be familiar with the fact that *The Pirates of Penzance* was given its première in New York in order to establish its copyright in the States and so as to prevent any repetition of what had happened with *H.M.S. Pinafore*, numerous pirated productions of which had been put on in the US because it had not been copyrighted there. It was not only popular stage shows which suffered – books did, too. You might think it strange that American piracy was still flourishing as late as the end of the nineteenth century in a world that was supposed to be civilised, but in fact a few unscrupulous American entrepreneurs continued the practice, even if to a limited extent, up to the time when the United States finally signed the Universal Copyright Convention. The Russians and the Japanese were also given to piracy, publishing translations of any books that appealed to them without any kind of permission being given or payment made. Again, signature of the UCC put an end to these activities.

Nowadays, piracy is alive and well and flourishing in the Far East. Unauthorised editions of many British and American books, in the original English, can be obtained in India, Taiwan, Korea, and a number of other countries, and unauthorised translations are also produced. Protests are made regularly by governments and organisations such as the Publishers Association, and individual publishers take the offenders to court (if they can find them), but the pirates can rarely be effectively stopped. Indeed, the only way that they will be controlled is if the governments of the countries where the pirated editions are produced decide that they will crack down really heavily on the pirates and put them out of business. Most of the countries concerned seem to have little will to take that kind of action, but, as already mentioned, good news has recently been received from China, which appears suddenly to have realised that copyright should not be disregarded, and is taking some steps towards eliminating piracy.

In the meantime, if you should become aware that your book has been pirated, which is a very serious infringement of your rights, you should immediately inform your publisher, who will no doubt take any measures available, though possibly with little hope of repairing the damage that has been done, let alone stopping and punishing the criminals responsible for it.

What is not copyright?

While most would-be authors find it easy to accept the concept that generally-known facts are not copyright (although the way that you express them may be) and that, in most cases, works by people who have been dead for more than fifty (soon to be seventy) years are equally free of copyright restrictions, it often worries them a great deal to find that ideas and titles and even their own names are not copyright.

The fact that there is no copyright in ideas often causes very considerable concern to those writers who dream up a book which they believe might be successful but who do not already have a publisher to whom they can submit the proposal. The tutors of Creative Writing tell these would-be authors how to do their market research and how to approach those publishers (or agents) who might possibly respond favourably to their ideas. And then the student almost invariably asks, 'But how can I be sure that they won't pinch the idea, and give it to one of their regular writers?' The answer is that you can't be sure, but that reputable publishers are not thieves (despite Thomas Campbell's assertion, 'Now Barabbas was a publisher'). Earlier in this chapter the question of a publisher stealing a whole typescript (or at least the plot of a novel or story or the facts in a non-fiction book) was considered and dismissed as unlikely in the extreme. It is impossible to be quite as didactic about ideas simply because they are less tangible, and while it may not happen very often that two authors will come up with exactly the same characters and twists and turns in a plot, or exactly the same sequence of facts and extrapolations from them, it is far from unknown for two people to have the same basic idea simultaneously; indeed it happens quite frequently. This, incidentally, is one of the reasons why you will often see newspaper reviews covering several newly-published books on exactly the same themes – there has been no collusion between the publishers, nor have they been the victims of industrial espionage (they don't normally indulge in a great deal of colluding, nor do they spy on one another). In her excellent book, *Writing for Radio*, Rosemary Horstmann suggests that there is some evidence for what she calls 'a climate of ideas', which leads to several people having the same idea simultaneously, and that may be exactly what has happened.

If you send your idea to a publisher who rejects it but subsequently brings out a book on exactly the same theme, there are at least three possible explanations of what has occurred. Firstly, there may be no question at all of your idea having been 'borrowed' and passed to the author of the published book. Instead, by the time that your suggestion for a book arrived in the publisher's office, the author in question had already had exactly the same idea as you and had got in first, or if the ideas were considered simultaneously, was preferred because of greater ability or experience than you as a writer, perhaps having a known name in the book world or having been published previously by the publisher concerned. And as an alternative to this possibility, it may have been the editor rather than the author who had had the same idea as yours and had commissioned another author to write the book – dreaming up new books and finding the authors to write them is one of the major functions of a publisher's editor. 'Then why,' you may ask, 'didn't the publisher tell me when rejecting mine that it was turned down because a similar book was already on the stocks?' It might, indeed, have been thoughtful of the publisher to write on those lines, but many firms just use a form letter for rejections, without adding any explanations.

The second feasible explanation is that an idea for a book which was not acceptable at the time that you submitted it may have become far more interesting to the publisher only a short while after. Why? Perhaps the firm's sales representatives have suggested that such a book is needed, or perhaps an editorial decision taken at a high level within the firm concerned has decreed that the output of books on the particular subject shall be increased, or for any number of other reasons which may not sound especially logical, but are the way the often whim-driven world of publishing can work. 'But,' you protest again, 'in that case, why didn't they come back to me and ask me to write the book?' As already suggested, a more experienced, 'name' author may have been preferred, or it may simply have been a case of your proposal having been totally forgotten, and when you realise that in a single year most publishers receive in excess of a thousand offers of books, or ideas for them, then it may be a little easier to understand such a lapse of memory.

The third explanation is that you are quite right, and your idea has in fact been purloined by an unscrupulous publisher. It is still a pretty unlikely possibility, and you will be very unlucky if it happens to you. Most publishers are reputable, and as has already been said, would not dream of consciously stealing an idea. What can you do if you get treated in this way? Very little, because ideas are not copyright.

Titles are not copyright either, so you can call your book whatever you like, even if your chosen title has been used previously by a different author. It may be a good thing, in order to avoid any duplication, to try to find out whether your title *has* appeared on a book recently (a friendly bookseller or librarian will check the lists of books in print), although if there is already a book by that name you may decide that it is not likely to conflict in any way with your own, and that you will therefore stick to your choice. Even if you carefully select a title which does not appear to have been used for at least several years, there is no guarantee that some other author hasn't also picked it for a new book which hasn't yet reached the bookseller's lists (although if both that book and your own are about to be published, one or other publisher may spot the duplication in announcements in the trade press in time for a change to be made – which was exactly how and why the title of E.M. Almedingen's autobiography was switched from *Yesterday Never Dies* to *Tomorrow Will Come*). But in the unfortunate situation of two books with the same title being made available at the same time, there is nothing that either author can do.

Although there is no copyright in titles, it is essential to avoid using those which have considerable celebrity. If you call your book *Wild Swans* or *The Rector's Wife*, Jung Chang, in the first case, or Joanna Trollope, in the second, and/or their publishers could sue you for 'passing off', which is the legal term for trying to persuade members of the public to buy something (i.e., your book) other than the well-known article (i.e., the famous book) which they think they are buying. It is assumed that this is your purpose, even if it is not. Mind you, you would be pretty stupid to choose a title which is already a household name, and your publisher would have been even thicker than you to let you go on using it. Although this warning usually applies to fairly unusual titles, such as *The Day of the Jackal* or *Some Other Rainbow*, and you would be fairly safe with something like the name of the subject of a biography – *Jane Austen: a Life* or, simply, *Wellington* – you may need to be careful if you use a title which, however simple and factual it may seem, is that of a standard work in the field.

As for your own name, alas, that is not copyright either, and neither are pseudonyms. So you can't complain if you discover that some other author has the same name or pseudonym as you, even if the other author is producing work which you believe, by its content or its quality, will harm your reputation because readers will believe, as a result of the similarity of name, that you wrote it. It's a shame, but there's nothing to be done, unless one of you is willing to change names. What is even more of a shame is if your own real name happens to be the same as that of a top bestselling author, who could sue you for passing off. It would be rotten of them to do so, but they could, especially if you were writing in a similar genre to their own. And if you are not writing the same kind of book as your famous namesake, you will probably disappoint a lot of readers – for instance, if you are called Jilly Cooper, and publish a demure little novel in which no one is unfaithful to anyone else and the action always stops at the bedroom door, then anyone who buys the book expecting the celebrated Jilly Cooper's usual raunchy style of story is going to be bitterly disappointed. Again, your publisher should have advised you to choose a pseudonym, even if it goes rather against your grain, or at the very least to use your second name or an initial so that you become, for instance, Jilly Elizabeth Cooper, or Elizabeth Cooper, or Jilly E. Cooper, or some other variation on that theme.

Something else which is not copyright is a Press Release. At least, in theory it *is* copyright and should carry a notice rescinding ownership and transferring it into the public domain so that it can be used as intended. In practice, the status of the document is made clear by the mere heading 'Press Release'.

Moral Rights

The Copyright, Designs and Patents Act of 1988 introduced for the first time the legal concept of a creative person's moral rights. It defined four Moral Rights, the first two of which – the right to be identified as author or director, and the right to object to derogatory treatment of one's work – are those generally meant when Moral Rights are referred to.

The remaining two rights are the right not to suffer false attribution and the right to privacy of certain photographs and films. The first of these means that it is illegal for anyone to say that you are the author of a given piece of work if you are not, and the second prevents a commissioned private photograph or film from being made public against the owner's wishes.

The Right of Paternity

The right to be identified as author or director is usually, if politically incorrectly, referred to as 'the right of paternity'. It lays it down that the author of a work has the right to be identified whenever the work is published, in whatever form (and similar provisions apply to the work of composers, artists, architects and the directors of films). However, the Act provides that, unlike the other Moral Rights, which exist without the need for any formalities, this right cannot be enforced unless the author, or other creator, has 'asserted' the right. In the case of written work, this assertion is carried out by the author requiring the publisher to print a formal notice in all copies of the book, and to insist that it should also be included in any sub-licensed editions or versions.

The standard wording which has been adopted is:

The right of (Author's Name) to be identified as the author
of this work has been asserted by him (her) in accordance
with the Copyright, Designs and Patents Act 1988.

It is a legal requirement that the author should sign his or her request to the publisher to insert such a notice. However, in practice, many publishers include a clause in their contracts covering the point, so that when the contract is signed, you are deemed to have signed the request. Other publishers will include the wording without a signature if the author simply puts it on one of the preliminary pages in the typescript, and others again will incorporate it automatically without expecting the author to make a special point of demanding that it should go in. It is, after all, no skin off their nose.

The Right of Integrity

The right to object to derogatory treatment of one's work is often referred to as 'the right of integrity', and it is concerned with any changes to the work which amount to distortion or mutilation or which would be otherwise prejudicial to the honour or reputation of the author or other creator. It cannot be used to protest about run-of-the-mill copy-editing, however much you may dislike what has been done, unless the changes have totally altered the sense of what you wrote, or have damaged your text in some other important way – in other words, you cannot complain about matters which, from a commonsense point of view, would be regarded as trivial.

As already mentioned, this right does not have to be 'asserted', but simply exists, because it concerns a fault by commission rather than, in the case of the right of identification, the possibility of a fault of omission.

It might be worth noting, by the way, that the Right of Integrity may not be of much use to you unless you have asserted the Right of Paternity, since, if your name is not shown as the author of the work, you can hardly complain that your reputation has been damaged by mutilation of the text.

Moral Rights are part of the law of this country, so their infringement can be punished in court, although this would not apply to any act to which the author has previously given consent. Moral Rights cannot be assigned to any other person or organisation, which may be some consolation if you have surrendered your copyright, but authors are entitled, if they so wish, to waive them and are frequently forced to do so by, for example, the BBC and other television companies, whose contracts always demand such a waiver.

This is surely against the intention of the law. Fortunately, most publishers take a more reasonable view and are prepared to respect the author's Moral Rights.

Provided that the author was alive when the Act came into force in 1988, the Rights of Paternity and Integrity, like Copyright, exist during the lifetime of the author and for fifty (soon to be seventy) years thereafter, while the right not to have work falsely attributed to you expires twenty years after your death. Although Moral Rights may not be assigned, after your death they do pass to your legatee(s).

Incidentally, the EU has not as yet made any proposals on the harmonisation of Moral Rights in the Community.

It is important to understand that the Rights of Paternity and Integrity are not applicable to work which is published in a news-paper or magazine, having been originally written for that purpose, nor do they normally apply to work published in an encyclopaedia or yearbook or other work of reference to which many authors contribute. Equally, you do not have these rights in anything that you write as part of your employment.

3
Public Lending Right

Public libraries

The first municipal public libraries in Britain were authorised by Act of Parliament in 1850. The movement took quite a time to get going, but by the early years of the twentieth century, any community of any size had its public library, and cities and towns were served not only by the central library, but by branches which reached the suburbs and outlying districts. By applying for a ticket, anyone could borrow books without charge (though the funds were, of course, provided by those who paid rates). The British public library system became the most extensive and well-run in the world, a repository of immediately available knowledge and entertainment without parallel, the glory of the book trade – and a millstone round its neck.

The problem for publishers is that the brilliantly successful public libraries have turned the British into a nation of book-borrowers rather than book-buyers – why buy a book when you can get it for nothing from the library? Of course, even without widely available libraries, booklovers don't always buy all the books they read, and never have done – we all have friends who are happy to lend us books from their shelves and we gladly reciprocate. But lending a book to a few friends is one thing, and lending it to possibly hundreds of people, as public libraries do, is another. For the publisher it means the sale of a single copy to the library, instead of perhaps a dozen or more to members of the public.

British publishers have grumbled about this in a restrained kind of way throughout the twentieth century, but have managed to survive, adjusting their print quantities and published prices to the demand, whether it came from bookshops or from libraries or from a combination of both.

To authors, on the other hand, comparatively few of whom become affluent from their writings, the situation appeared to be remarkably unfair. To receive a royalty of a few pence on a single copy of a book which might then be read by scores of borrowers seemed not far short of daylight robbery – the stealing of their talent, of their ability to entertain or to instruct. And what made it worse, until quite a long time after World War II, was that the royalty was often less than that paid on the sale of a copy of the book in a bookshop; publishers sold unbound sheets to firms called 'library suppliers', who then put them into substantial bindings which could be expected to extend the life of the book through far more borrowings than the publishers' bindings would have allowed (even in the days when genuine cloth was used), and since a set of sheets was sold for less than the published price of the complete book, the royalty was reduced.

The history of Public Lending Right in Britain

The first public muttering by an author to the effect that a payment should be made for the borrowing of a book from a public library came as early as 1909 from the children's writer, Eric Leyland. No one took much notice, and it was not until 1951, by which time the number of libraries and of annual borrowings had vastly increased, that the novelist John Brophy crystallised the desire of most authors to receive some extra compensation for the almost entirely unrewarded reading of the library copies of their books. He put forward the idea of 'the Brophy Penny', a proposed payment to the author of 1d (the pre-decimalisation penny, now worth in real terms not less than 10p) to be made for each time that a book was borrowed from a public library. There was some support for this principle, not surprisingly from the Society of Authors, but notably from A.P. Herbert, well known at that time as an author, a Member of Parliament, and a committed fighter against some of the more absurd injustices of the law. There was also considerable opposition, especially from people who said that authors were jolly lucky to have so many sales to libraries anyway, and what were they complaining about? A tiny number of extremely successful authors saw no necessity for any such scheme, and most librarians were strongly against it. And there was little agreement about whether the money should come from the central government, from the rates, or from the borrowers. Publishers joined the argument, saying, not surprisingly, that if there were to be any such payment, they should have a share in it.

Twenty-eight years were to pass between John's Brophy's suggestion of the Brophy Penny and the passing of the law which established Public Lending Right (PLR). During that period the idea that some payment should be made to authors for library borrowing was espoused by various politicians and opposed by others; a great many different methods of assessing and administering payments were discussed; six different Bills were presented to Parliament, all of which failed; and over the years the issue alternated between being live and apparently moribund. John Brophy died in 1965, and A.P. Herbert in 1971, both without having seen success in this matter, but both with the consolation that it was firmly on the political agenda. The other campaigners had not given up and by 1971 it seemed that the government, of whatever political colour, would eventually have to bring in a bill – if only someone could decide exactly how the whole thing should work.

The issue dragged on. In 1972, determined to press for a resolution of the problem, a band of authors, calling themselves Writers' Action Group and led by Maureen Duffy, and John Brophy's daughter, Brigid Brophy, joined the battle. The vigour of the campaign they led, and the support of Ted Willis in the Lords and of Andrew Faulds, Michael Foot, Hugh Jenkins and Norman St John Stevas in the Commons, finally won the day, and despite some last-ditch efforts by its opponents, the Bill was passed, and by March 22nd 1979 had received the Royal Assent.

Of course, authors did not receive any immediate benefit. The scheme could clearly not be set up overnight, and it took another four years before it was operative and the first payments were made. At the time that the Bill was passed, the government had allocated an annual sum of £2 million to cover both the administration and the payments to authors. In the early months of 1984, Public Lending Rights accounts went out to the 7562 authors who had registered. Almost fifteen hundred of them received nothing, because insufficient loans of their books had been recorded, but the remaining six thousand were happy to find that their bank balances had been increased. The rate paid was 1.02p per loan. A limit of £5000 for any one author had been set, and 46 authors received that maximum amount. Almost two-thirds of the registered authors received somewhere between £1 and £9. Better than nothing, but hardly a fortune, and many authors complained that no increase had been made in the funding despite the fact that inflation had been high between 1979 and 1984. The sum currently available (1995) is £4 936 000, and the rate per loan has gone up to 2p. 24 326 authors were registered in 1994 – more than three times as many as in 1984 – of whom 110 received the present maximum of £6000, while 13 902 were in the £1-£99 bracket, and nearly five thousand unfortunates got nothing.

Who qualifies to receive PLR?

Any author who is resident in the United Kingdom and has had a book published which is available in Britain is entitled to apply for Public Lending Right. The publisher need not be a recognised commercial concern – if you have self-published your work, you can apply. Of course, whether any money will be received depends firstly on whether there are any copies of the book in public libraries, and secondly whether they are borrowed sufficiently often over the twelve-month period to bring in the minimum payment, which for any author is a total of £1 (that is to say, fifty borrowings at the present rate of 2p), whether that sum is made up of payments for one book or many.

Artists who have illustrated a book or books can also register for PLR. Agreement will have to be reached between the author and artist as to how the payments will be shared between them. In the same way, if a book has more than one author, they must agree how the moneys will be split.

Originally, editors and translators were excluded from the scheme, but they have been eligible since 1985, and books by more than three authors were also included as from 1991. No PLR is paid in respect of reference books which are consulted in public libraries but not taken out on loan, but plans for the remuneration of authors of such books are currently under discussion and will probably be implemented if a fair method of assessing their use can be devised.

In order to get yourself and your books on to the PLR computer, you must obtain a form from:

Public Lending Right Office,
Bayheath House,
Prince Regent Street,
Stockton-on-Tees,
Cleveland TS18 1DF

This is something that you must do yourself. It is not a job for your publisher or even your agent. Neither of them has any share in your PLR earnings, which are paid directly to you, so it is unreasonable to expect them to undertake the chore of registration on your behalf. Not that it is much of a chore. The form is clear and easy to fill in – the main requirement, apart from name and address, title and publisher of the book(s), and information about where any moneys are to be sent, is the inclusion of ISBNs (International Standard Book Numbers), because they are the principal means of identification of the books which are borrowed.

ISBNs, which can be used worldwide to identify not only a book but also its country of origin and its publisher, are allocated by the publisher, and a new number is given to each new edition of the work. ISBNs are normally clearly shown on the jacket or cover of the book, and on the imprint page (usually on the back, or verso, of the title page). If you should self-publish a book it is not a legal requirement that it should have an ISBN, but it is advisable, and essential if your book goes into public libraries and you want it to earn PLR – books without ISBNs are not eligible for the scheme. You can apply for an ISBN – no charge is made – for any book that you self-publish by writing to:

The ISBN Agency,
Whitaker & Sons Ltd,
12 Dyott Street,
London WC1A 1DF.

One point worth remembering is that libraries nowadays have paperbacks on their shelves as well as hardcover books, and there are also increasing numbers of large print editions, so that one book may appear in many different formats, each with a different ISBN; if your book is available in more than one edition you should give the PLR registrars details of all of them; equally, if a revised edition of a book is produced it will be given a new ISBN, and you will need to notify the PLR office accordingly. If you have any difficulty with the form, you will find that the Registrar and the staff at the PLR office are extremely helpful.

The PLR registration lists close on June 30th each year, so it is a good idea to get all your books listed before then. However, you should include only those titles which will have already been published by the closing date.

How does PLR work?

The age of computers would appear to have made the assessment of PLR a comparatively simple matter, but even so the payments are based on notional rather than actual figures. The analysis of 576 000 000 loans a year would be a pretty Herculean task, and in any case not all public libraries have yet acquired the necessary equipment to supply the required data in full. To begin with, then, from all the library authorities up and down the country which are able to supply full records, a different group of thirty is chosen each year. These libraries are situated in various parts of Great Britain and Northern Ireland, including both urban and rural districts, and some of them supply information from their branches as well as from the main library. The figures of all loans from these sample libraries, broken down by ISBN, are then multiplied in proportion to regional lending figures, and the regional totals are then added together to give an estimate of the total loans for each book – the notional figure on which the payments are made. The figures reported in 1994 reflect fifteen and a half million loans, which is no more than 2.69% of the total actual loans. It may seem a small sample, but is in fact large enough to provide a reliable set of figures, especially since various safeguards are built in to prevent the manipulation of the results (for instance, by authors persuading their friends to borrow their books repeatedly from one of the reporting libraries).

That there are flaws in the system has never been denied. One of the complaints which has been most frequently voiced is that no account is taken of the time for which a borrower has kept the book before returning it to the library. Not surprisingly, those who are most concerned about this are authors of very long books, but they are joined by other writers, such as those who produce manuals, who claim that even though their books may be quite short, they are kept out on average for longer periods than books which are purely entertainment, because readers find the advice they give so valuable. You can see the point in either case. A book like *A Suitable Boy*, Vikram Seth's enormous novel, is not likely to be read as many times in a year, simply because of its length, as a 45 000 word romance, and any book of instruction is likely to require more study than a short novel. The argument can be extended to cover a wide variety of books, but there are far too many imponderables when you come to examine questions of that sort to make it easy to feel that the system should be changed: some readers are quicker than others; some keep a book out not because they are still reading it, but because they forget to return it, or are ill or can't take it back for some other reason; and of course, equally, there are many people who take a book out of the library and return it straight away, deciding that they don't like it, or remembering that they've read it before; and so on. And the worst problem is that if PLR payments were weighted according to the length of the book, lines would have to be drawn – would it be any fairer than the present system to rule that a book of, say, 49 000 words should receive a smaller payment than one of 50 000 words? And (a prospect not to be considered without alarm) authors might be tempted to pad their books in order to get the higher rate, resisting any attempt by publishers to cut the unnecessary verbiage. If you look at any arguments about the length of borrowing-time, whether based on the length of the book or on some other criterion, you will find yourself making value judgments – and that's a real minefield.

Another complaint concerns the top earners. In February 1994, 116 authors earned the top figure of £6000. 'Scandalous!' say some, who point out that these are best-selling authors who don't need the money anyway, and wouldn't it be better to distribute it among the less fortunate writers. Back to value judgments again. And on the other side are some who point out that if the majority of these high earners were paid on their actual loans instead of being restricted to a maximum amount of £6000, they would earn a great deal more, and even if they don't really need it, they are entitled to get their full share.

All that can be said in the end is that PLR as it exists is reasonably fair to most authors, that the PLR Registrar (currently Dr James Parker) and his staff are constantly refining their system to make it more comprehensive, more accurate, and less expensive to run. The one major change which every author would welcome would be a greater sum of money being allocated by the Government to fund PLR, a move which is due not only because the real value of the present £5 million has been reduced by inflation to far less than that of the original £2 million allocated, but because even in 1979 £2 million was inadequate. That £2 million had to pay for the setting up of the system and for the payments due to six thousand authors; nowadays, £5 million has to be shared (after expenses, which truly are kept to a minimum) among about three times as many authors; in real terms the 2.0p per loan paid for the year ending June 1994 is very much less than the 1.02p paid in 1984. You might say that this is only to be expected when more and more authors register themselves and their books, but surely all should be fairly recompensed. The trouble is that no British government does much for the Arts, and Literature is particularly badly supported. Perhaps we shall see an improvement now that we have a national lottery.

Foreign PLR

Britain is not alone in having PLR, although the system may differ from country to country. Sweden and Denmark both had relevant laws in place a long time before our 1979 Act, and indeed not only was their experience used in framing the details of our law, but the mere fact that they had felt it just to compensate authors for library borrowings helped to influence the British politicians who eventually passed that law. Schemes also exist in a number of other European countries, and in Australia, Canada and New Zealand. (Incidentally, British authors receive less on average than other countries pay their writers.)

When our PLR first started, it was available only to British authors resident in the UK. On the other hand, the system which was introduced in what was at that time West Germany allowed of payments to foreign writers, and since this was good news for British authors, it seemed only fair that, as well as permitting foreign writers who are resident in Britain to participate in our PLR, we should extend the right and its benefits to West German authors. This was done some years ago, but only with Germany, as it now is, do we have this reciprocal arrangement. (It may be of interest, by the way, that German PLR regulations differ from ours in withholding, for cultural purposes, a proportion of the moneys available, after which it pays authors 70% and publishers 30% of the loan rate.)

The PLR moneys from Germany which are due to British authors, and which amount in total to some £80 000 a year, cannot, under the German regulations, be paid direct to those authors. Instead, they are paid in bulk to the Authors' Licensing and Collecting Society Ltd (ALCS), which then distributes the cash to the recipients concerned, minus a minimal handling charge.

ALCS was set up in 1977, on the model of similar collecting societies which have existed much longer on the Continent. It is not a government agency, but is run by and for authors, its affairs being controlled by a twelve-person Council of Management, consisting of four nominees each from the Society of Authors and the Writers' Guild of Great Britain, and four elected ALCS members. It has a membership of several thousand authors, and a currently expanding professional staff, needed to cope with the substantial sums which the Society processes. As well as collecting foreign PLR funds, it also administers the distribution of moneys due to authors from photocopying licences and from foreign use of British television material via satellite and cable.

It is worth pointing out that the German PLR authorities do not hand over the money for those British authors who are not members of ALCS, retaining any such sums in a fund until such time as membership is taken out. So, just as all authors should register with the British PLR office as soon as they have had a book published, they should also join ALCS. The current annual subscription is £5 (excluding VAT) and details may be obtained from:

The Membership Secretary,
ALCS,
33/34 Alfred Place,
London WC1E 7DP.

Members of the Society of Authors and the Writers' Guild are automatically enrolled in ALCS without payment of a fee.

It is very much to be hoped that the idea of PLR will be more and more widely adopted throughout the world. Within the European Union, only Britain, Germany, Denmark (which pays Danish authors only), the Netherlands and Greece (which has virtually no public libraries anyway) have PLR systems, but recent EU rules have laid down that the principle of payments to authors for library loans (including audio-visual material, sheet music, works of art, etc. – indeed anything which public libraries lend out, provided it is in copyright) should be embodied in the laws of all member countries by 1st July 1995. How this will be implemented, and whether British authors will benefit from foreign schemes, remains to be seen. Initially, any new systems will probably apply only to nationals of the country concerned, but once PLR is recognised and implemented in all member countries of the EU, and indeed world-wide, it is likely that in due course it will be widened so as to apply to all borrowed authors, regardless of their nationality or place of residence. British authors should then do particularly well, partly because of the large market for them in the English-speaking countries of the world, and partly because in foreign-language countries English books are not only frequently translated, but are widely read in the original tongue.

It is very probable that, as other countries adopt the general principle of PLR, they will also follow the German precedent of payment in bulk to a central agency. ALCS is, of course, already in place, and will be capable of handling any such additional distributions – and will no doubt prove to be a model for other countries needing to set up a similar organisation.

4
Photocopying

The ubiquitous photocopying machine

If you accept the idea that authors should be paid when their books are borrowed from public libraries, you may agree that the principle should be extended to any borrowing at all. But of course it is quite impractical to think of making any charge on behalf of the author when a private individual lends a book (or a magazine, for that matter) to a friend. At least someone bought the book or magazine in the first place, it is not being offered as a service to which the friend has a right, and even if it has passed through a whole string of borrowers – well, that's the way things are and always have been. It cannot really be considered as an infringement of copyright.

In recent years, however, a different kind of problem has arisen as a result of the explosion in technology that has taken place. The machine which causes the problem is the photocopier (the copying that it does is known as reprography). You can go to the library and use its photocopying machine to make a copy of an entire book, or several copies of part or all of it, or, if you think that a librarian might stop you, you can borrow the book from the library and take it to a copyshop, where there will probably be no problem. Or if you are a teacher you can photocopy part or all of a textbook so that everyone in the class has a copy at the cost of a few pence. Or if you are running a major company and you think that all your staff, numbering several hundred, should read a certain article which you have seen in a magazine, you can photocopy it on the firm's machine and distribute it without having to buy a single extra copy of the original. Or if you run an amateur drama group you can buy one copy of the play you are about to put on and photocopy as many other copies as you need for the cast and backstage staff, which will be a lot cheaper than getting them from the publisher. Yes, you can do all those things, but you most certainly shouldn't.

How much photocopying is legal?

The amount of photocopying that you, the reader of this book – or anyone else for that matter – can do without permission is strictly limited. You can make a single copy of part of a book, or a single copy of a single magazine article. The proportion of the book that you photocopy must be no more than 'reasonable', and any photocopy you make must be for use for research or private study. (What is 'reasonable'? You may well ask, because the term is not easy to define. Probably no more than one chapter, or even less.) And why are you restricted to so small an amount of photocopying? Because, unless it is your own work or that of someone who died more than fifty years ago, the photocopying is likely to be a use of the author's copyright material, and if anyone ought to respect an author's copyright it is another author, or would-be author.

That probably sounds simple enough, but it is not all. It is not the copyright of authors only which may be infringed by photocopying – the publisher has rights in the matter too, and indeed, in the case of a magazine, the publisher often owns all the rights.

So what happens if you want to photocopy more than a 'reasonable' amount of the book or more than one article from a magazine? The first answer is that you should go out and buy yourself a copy of whatever it may be so that you don't have to photocopy at all. But this may not be practical, especially if the work in question is out of print, and the procedure then is to seek permission for whatever photocopying you want to do from the copyright owner or his or her representative (the publisher, in most cases). This permission will probably be given, if the work is out of print, but sometimes a fee will be charged.

The Copyright Licensing Agency

Most of the photocopying that you as an author are likely to want to do is really small beer, comparable in many ways to the lending of a book by a private individual to a friend. What copyright owners, and this may include you, are really concerned about is the widespread photocopying of material, often in very large quantities, which goes on in schools, colleges, universities, government offices, and business concerns (especially those with large staffs). In some cases, it is understandable that the user wants to photocopy rather than to buy quantities of the book in question – especially in schools, which are so often short of cash for such purposes. And if publishers were to insist that the only answer is the purchase of books, the users would probably photocopy anyway, illegally, and would often get away with it.

To cope with this problem an organisation called the Copyright Licensing Agency Ltd (CLA) was set up in 1982. It is owned and controlled jointly by the Authors' Licensing and Collection Society

(ALCS) and the Publishers Licensing Society (PLS). The work of the CLA is to issue licences permitting the licensees to photocopy copyright material on payment of a small fee. The modesty of the amounts charged is comparable to the minimal loan rate paid under the PLR system, but the sums are seen by the users to be reasonable, and that is an important point in persuading them to observe the law. In setting up the CLA, the representatives of the Society of Authors and the Writers' Guild on the Management Council of ALCS, as with PLR, insisted that the authors' shares of the photocopying licence fees which would be collected should be paid to them directly, rather than through publishers or agents. The proportions in which the fees would be split between author and publisher would depend on the terms of the contract. In most cases, for books the arrangement is a 50/50 one.

How does the CLA work?

The first thing that has to happen before the CLA can operate effectively is for it to be mandated by the copyright owners to act on their behalf in the licensing of photocopying and the collection of the fees. In effect, an author (who is usually the copyright owner) when signing a contract is usually presented nowadays with a clause requiring him or her to delegate to the publisher the right to issue such a mandate. It is done this way because it is easier for the publisher to give a blanket mandate, covering all the titles on the firm's list than for each author to have to give an individual mandate. Most publishers have given these comprehensive mandates.

Having secured the mandates, the CLA begins its work by approaching educational authorities and other large concerns, pointing out to them that photocopying on a substantial scale for professional use is an infringement of copyright and therefore illegal, and then suggesting that a licence could be issued which would allow such photocopying on payment of an appropriate fee. In some cases, it has been comparatively easy to persuade the relevant controlling bodies to take out licences, but there are still many grey areas. Public libraries have photocopying machines, and prominently displayed by them are notices pointing out how much photocopying of books can legally be done, but it is not practical to keep a librarian permanently on duty to see that no photocopying member of the public breaks the rules and infringes someone's copyright. Although the CLA makes considerable efforts to persuade copyshops of the need to conform to the law, it is extremely difficult to convince them that in certain cases they should turn away business in order to protect the copyright of some author or other. And industrial photocopiers have been less than eager to sign on as licensees.

Nevertheless, the CLA has had a great deal of success in exercising control over the immense amount of infringing photocopying that goes on, and it continues to widen the scope of its activities to bring more and more users within the law.

The institutions taking out the licences which the CLA issues are required to report back with details of what they have photocopied. In some cases, known as 'collective users' (mostly education authorities whose licence covers all the schools and colleges in their area and within their jurisdiction), a blanket fee is paid and a sampling system is used to list the works photocopied, in rather the same way as PLR operates in the libraries. 'Transactional users', on the other hand, whose scope is less wide, are required to keep accurate records of all photocopying by title, author, publisher and ISBN or ISSN (International Standard Serial Number – a numbering system similar to ISBNs but applied to magazines and journals rather than books), and to pay a fee per page.

All the data is fed back to the CLA, which then distributes the fees it has collected, sending half the available moneys in respect of books to PLS and half to ALCS, together with the detailed information which allows these organisations to share out the sums received between the publishers and authors concerned in appropriate amounts. In the case of magazines, especially learned and academic journals, all the moneys go to the publishers, who have a legal claim on the whole amount, although the ALCS representatives on the CLA board campaign constantly to persuade the magazine and journal publishers to accept that this is unjust and that the authors should receive a share of the income.

The amounts which the CLA distributes are not to be sneezed at. Naturally, in the early years, the sums which came in were small, and out of them the administration had to be paid for (although it must be said that the organisation is run with admirable economy). However, by the time that the CLA was ready for the first distribution, part paid in 1987 and the rest in 1988, the sum available was no less than £1.4 million. Since then distributions have been made half-yearly, and the total paid out to date at the time of writing is over £16 million, which gives an average of £2.3 million per year. That figure is expected to increase substantially as more photocopying is licensed – indeed, the figure for 1992/3 topped £4 million, and that for 1993/4 was well over £4.5 million. The total amount so far paid to ALCS for distribution to authors is a little over £7 million (less than half all CLA's payments because, as already explained, publishers of magazines and learned and academic journals do not share the income with their authors). It is not surprising, of course, that by far the largest share of the money in respect of books goes to the publishers and authors of non-fiction, which is, after all, more likely to be photocopied for educational or informational purposes or for research than fiction.

Photocopying internationally

Britain is not alone in having an organisation like the CLA which collects fees for the photocopying of copyright material. Currently sixteen other countries have licensing arrangements, including the United States of America and most of the members of the EU. The majority of them, like the CLA, are members of IFRRO (International Federation of Reproduction Rights Organisations), and many of them have reciprocal arrangements with their counterparts in other countries, a development to which the CLA gives some priority, especially when concerned with English-speaking countries. The result is that the sums distributed by the CLA include quite substantial payments received for overseas photocopying of British material, while amounts in the region of a quarter of a million pounds go overseas annually to foreign publishers and authors whose works have been photocopied in Britain.

Despite the growth of international co-operation in respect of illegal photocopying, it is interesting to note that the European Union has not so far announced any plans for the harmonisation of reprographic policies within the member countries.

5
Permissions

Using copyright material

The fact that your own written work is copyright, and will remain so for fifty (or, soon, seventy) years after your death, means that for quite a long time to come no one else may use it, or any part of it, in any way, without being given permission to do so either by yourself or by someone to whom you have delegated the right to authorise such use. This also applies to unpublished work, and to letters, which, to the surprise of many people, are the copyright of the writer, not of the recipient, although the latter may own the physical letter itself. And since the labourer is always worthy of his or her hire, even if the actual labour of writing was done a long time ago, you will in many cases be entitled to a fee.

The corollary to this is that you may not use anyone else's copyright material without permission. Although occasionally a publisher will agree to obtain any necessary permissions for you, this is rare, and normally it is your responsibility, and one to be taken seriously, since use of someone else's material without permission could result in damages being awarded against you.

Curiously, some authors feel that it is possible to quote from a book which is out of print, or one which has been published only in a foreign country, without obtaining permission, despite the fact that the author is still alive or has not been dead for the necessary length of time to make the work out of copyright. Copyright is not affected by whether or not the book is available, nor, in almost all cases, by the nationality of the author.

But do you have to get permission for everything you quote, even if it is only a few words? No. There is no problem with material which is out of copyright – quote away to your heart's content (though be careful if your source is an edited version of the original work, because the editor may sometimes be able to claim copyright). There are also circumstances in which you can quote copyright material without needing to gain permission, if it comes under the heading of what the 1988 Copyright Act calls 'fair dealing for purposes of criticism or review'. Although the Act neither defines that phrase nor expands on it, 'criticism or review' is clear enough, if somewhat restrictive; however, it is generally taken that you may also quote for the purpose of illustrating a point, or backing up an argument that you are putting forward (or presenting a contrary view). The amount of someone else's text that you may use in such ways is naturally limited, and the Society of Authors and the Publishers Association agreed jointly some years ago, quite a while before the present Copyright Act, that the following lengths of extract would be considered to come under the heading of 'fair dealing': a single extract from a prose work should not be longer than 400 words, while a series of extracts, none of which should exceed 300 words, should not total more than 800 words; an extract of up to 40 lines from a poem is permissible, provided that this is not more than a quarter of the poem.

These standards are still applicable, especially if you are quoting, as the Act says 'for purposes of criticism or review'. If you use material to illustrate a point or in presenting views for or against an argument, you almost certainly need to restrict the amount of quoted material for it to qualify as 'fair dealing' – a sentence or two, or even a couple of paragraphs, may be all right, but could sometimes be regarded as an infringement, depending on the way in which you are using the quote and on its source. You need to consider such matters as the proportion of space that any extract(s) will take up in relation to your own work, and whether your work is directly competitive with the source of your quotation, and whether it might be felt that you were using the quoted material simply to save you the bother of writing on the subject yourself. You have to be reasonable about it, and it might help if you tried to imagine how you would feel about it if the quoted work were your own – would you be happy, or would you feel that advantage of you had been taken? If you have any doubts at all, especially if you are quoting poetry, it is wise to seek permission .

Of course, in quoting any material under the heading of 'fair dealing' you must still acknowledge the source of the quotation, giving both the author's name and the title of the book, and preferably the publisher too (see also p.55).

'Fair dealing' does not, by the way, apply to anthologies, for which you need permission for even the shortest of quotations if the material is in copyright. And there is an obligation to state, when applying for permission, that the material is to be used in an anthology.

Obtaining permission

If the amount of copyright material that you want to use exceeds the length permitted under 'fair dealing', you will need to apply for permission. This applies whether it is a quotation from a published or unpublished work, prose or poetry, or a photograph or painting, or a letter. The first step is to check that the material is actually in copyright, remembering that if whoever created it has been dead for fifty (seventy) years, the copyright has expired. Next you will need to find out who owns the copyright, or, more frequently, who controls it – the copyright in most books belongs to the author, but if the book has been published the right to quote from it is almost always controlled by the publisher of the original edition. (If you are looking at a paperback, a glance at the printing history, usually to be found on the back of the title page, will give you the name of the publisher who first brought the book out – often not the paperback publisher.) So you then write to the publisher, detailing the material which you want to reproduce, and asking permission to do so. It is important to describe the kind of book that you are writing, and if you already have a publisher for your work, you should include that information too. The publisher will normally respond with an indication of the fee which will be payable and details of the form which the acknowledgment should take, but if for some reason, such as the rights having reverted, the publisher is no longer in a position to grant permission, your request will probably be passed to the author or to his or her agent.

An application for permission to use copyright material may sometimes result in a demand for full details about the use which is to be made of it, including perhaps sight of your manuscript, or that part of it which includes the material to be quoted. Obviously, the copyright owner in such a case is anxious lest his or her work is to be quoted in such a way as to ridicule it, or distort it by taking it out of context. Some authors are very much opposed to any extract being taken from their works – this is particularly true of poets, who may not object to a complete poem being used, whether in an anthology or otherwise, but will not look kindly on someone who wants to quote just a few lines from it. You could, perhaps, cite 'fair dealing', but only, of course, if the extract meets the restrictions on length and you are using it for purposes of criticism or review. If in the end permission is refused, there is nothing you can do about it, except perhaps to give the gist of the material in your own words, attributing them to the author whom you wish to quote, but being extremely careful not to quote him or her directly.

It is possible that you may fail totally to find the owner of the copyright (although the search should not be given up too easily). In that case you will have either to omit the quoted passage, or to insert a notice in the book saying that you have tried unsuccessfully to trace the copyright owner (keep copies of all the letters you have sent, so that, if necessary, you can prove your diligence) and that anyone claiming ownership should get in touch with you, via your publisher. If the copyright owner does contact you, you will probably have to pay a fee, but this notice will, with any luck, save you from an accusation of plagiarism.

But supposing that what you want to quote or reproduce is not in book form? If it is an extract from a television programme, you would apply to the BBC or the ITV company concerned. If you want to quote a lyric from a song you would apply to the publisher of the sheet music or perhaps to the company which has produced the record. For a photograph you will normally need to find out who the photographer is, or to apply to his or her employer (which might be a newspaper, for instance), or to go to one of the photographic agencies. It is wise to seek the publisher's advice before making any application for permission to use a photograph, so as to ensure that you get the right kind of clearance (for instance, the form in which the material is to be used and the territories in which the book is to be published will affect the matter). It is no longer the case, incidentally, since the passing of the 1988 Copyright Act, that someone who commissions a photographer to take a picture owns the copyright in it. Nowadays copyright always belongs to the photographer – so if you, as an author, go and pay a local photographer to have a portrait photograph taken, perhaps for publicity purposes, you will have to get the photographer's permission to use the picture in that way.

When to apply for permission

It is not absolutely necessary to apply for permission until your book has been accepted for publication, and indeed, it may be wise to leave it until that point for a number of reasons: firstly, your publisher may in editing the book suggest that you should cut the quotation, and there is no point in spending time and trouble, and possibly paying a fee, if the material is not to be used; secondly, the publisher will be able to advise you as to the territory for which you need to obtain permission – it is not always necessary to pay for the right to reproduce the copyright material throughout the world, especially if your book is unlikely to be published outside Britain, and it will be cheaper to apply for permission for a more restricted territory; thirdly, some organisations, when granting permission for the use of copyright material, quote a fee which must be paid within a limited period, and state that if they do not receive the specified payment within that time a further application for permission to use the material will have to be made, and the fee will then be increased (which seems very unjust, but is not illegal).

On the other hand, you may wish to know as soon as possible whether or not you are going to be given permission to use the material (you cannot assume that it will always be granted), and whether you will be able to afford the fee. If for some reason you cannot include the material, you may have to do quite a bit of rearrangement and rewriting.

Whether you should apply for permission to quote copyright material at an early stage or only when the book has been accepted is a question which depends on circumstances and which you must answer for yourself. But you should certainly not leave an application to the last minute. If the book has been set up in print, it may be very costly to make changes if permission is refused. And, of course, there can be considerable delay if the copyright owner is difficult to trace or if your request has to be handed on by the original publisher perhaps to the agent and then to the author or the author's heirs. Such a hold-up may cause all sorts of difficulties for your own publisher, especially if the publication schedule for the book is fairly tight.

Fees

It is impossible to lay down any scale of charges for the use of copyright material, since they can vary enormously. Some publishers will set a fee in accordance with the type of work in which the quoted material will appear, asking for a smaller amount for a book which will have a very small print quantity than for a more popular publication, and perhaps not even charging if the book's profits are to be given to charity.

The fees can often be quite high, particularly if the words quoted are by a famous person, and if you want to reproduce a Picasso painting in your book you may well find that the cost is prohibitive. One kind of quotation is particularly expensive, and that is an extract from the lyrics of a song, for which those who control the copyright always seem to want an exorbitant sum, even for a couple of lines.

Fees also depend on the nature of the quoted material – the charge for a complete poem of 20 lines may be a lot higher than an extract of 20 lines from a longer work – and on the use to which the quoted material is put – fees for quotation in an anthology are usually steeper than if the lines are to be used in an illustrative or critical way within the text of a book.

The question of whether the author or the publisher pays permission fees cannot be answered simply. It depends on circumstances. In the main, authors are expected to accept responsibility for clearance and for payment, especially where textual matter is concerned, but publishers are sometimes willing to pay the fees for photographs. However, it is always worth trying to negotiate on the whole question of permission expenses, since in certain circumstances – if, for instance, the costs are likely to be substantial – the publisher will sometimes agree to contribute towards them, or even to pay them all, and this applies particularly in the case of anthologies. Whatever the cost is likely to be, and whatever the problems, the whole matter should be discussed with the publisher, in detail, at the time that the contract for the book is negotiated. If the publisher does agree to bear some or all of the costs, any payment made to the author in this respect should not be in the form of an increase in the advance, but should be an entirely separate amount. Publishers will often help the author with advice about obtaining permissions, and may even supply the author with forms to use in the applications.

The publisher may ask to see evidence that permissions have been obtained, even if you have signed a clause in the agreement asserting that you would be responsible for clearing the right to include any copyright material other than your own. This is a reasonable request, since the publishing company will probably get more severely clobbered than you if your book contains copyright material for the inclusion of which permission has not been obtained. In any case, you will need to keep copies of the permission documents, since you will be able to claim the fees for tax purposes against your earnings on the book, and, of course, so that you can prove at any future date that you have clearance.

Acknowledgments

One of the requirements of the Copyright Act is that 'a sufficient acknowledgement' should accompany any quoted work, and as well as paying a fee for the use of the material, the copyright owner will invariably ask that a statement of its source (usually the title of the book, the author and the publisher, and sometimes the date of publication, too) and of the person or firm granting the permission should be included in your book. The details can sometimes be incorporated into your text, but it is more usual and convenient to print any such acknowledgments in the preliminary pages of the book, or at the end of it. Except in the unusual case of the publisher having agreed to clear all permissions, it will be your responsibility to ensure that all the relevant details are given to the publisher for inclusion before the book goes to press.

A further requirement of the copyright owner, in some cases, is that you should supply one or more copies of your book when it is printed, and this applies particularly, but not exclusively, in the case of anthologies; this condition amounts, in fact, to an increase in the fee charged, since you will have to pay for the extra copies of the book. While that is perhaps reasonable in the case of an anthology (it is something that you should be prepared for and which you should have discussed with your publisher, so that perhaps some special arrangements may be made), it can seem somewhat unfair if your book is not an anthology and the material quoted is not a substantial part of it; one copy for the grantor of the permission might be all right, but you could argue, gently, if more are asked for.

6
Agents

The relationship between authors and agents

Many would-be authors believe that it is vital to have an agent if you want to get published, and that you won't succeed without one. It isn't true. Agents are mostly nice things to have – 83% of authors responding to a recent survey thought their agents were smashing (or, at least, not at all bad) – but they are certainly not essential. Roughly 50% of the members of the Society of Authors, all published writers, get along quite happily without employing an agent. It has to be said that the 50% includes a number of writers working in educational and academic fields, in which it is unusual to use an agent, but that still leaves a great many Society of Authors members, producing books of various genres, both fiction and non-fiction, who sell their work to publishers direct. Admittedly, a few publishers deal only with agents and will not even look at unagented typescripts, but they are a very small minority, and most publishers will readily sign up authors direct (indeed, many prefer to work that way). In any case, it is often more difficult to persuade an agent to take you on than to find a publisher who will publish your book.

Incidentally, the majority of agents deal with most kinds of books, and that includes both fiction and non-fiction. Some of them may exclude certain categories, such as children's books, and others specialise in various genres. Full details can be found in *Writers' and Artists' Yearbook*.

However, if you do have an agent, what are your rights as far as he or she is concerned? The first thing to remember is that the agent is employed by you. You pay him or her a percentage of your earnings from the work that he or she has handled for you – 10%, or sometimes 15% (any higher percentage is excessive) of your earnings from British publication of the work, and rather higher sums on the proceeds from the sale of US and foreign language rights which he/she, or his/her sub-agent, has arranged. In return you are entitled to expect quite a lot: firstly, that the agent will have a substantial knowledge of publishing and the current publishing scene; and then that he or she will do a good job of selling your work for you; will check your agreements before you sign them and your royalty statements before accepting them; will chase the publisher over any matter in which there has been any failure to do all that is expected; will advise you of your rights, and if there is cause for complaint, or you have a dispute with your publisher, will handle the matter on your behalf, acting not only as your advocate but as a buffer between you and the person with whom you would otherwise yourself be arguing; will possibly secure commissions for you; and will probably also offer you what might be called 'career guidance', editorial advice, and friendship. Most agents do all those things as a matter of course, so it is no wonder that their authors (whom they tend to call 'clients') think they're splendid.

A particularly important part of the service that the agent offers is availability. Publishers are genuinely extremely busy people, and may not always be available to talk at length with the author or to engage in regular communication, and the author can do little to change that situation. Because, on the other hand, the relationship between an author and an agent is somewhat different, the author has a right to expect the agent to be available, to communicate, to give advice and information whenever the author wants it. Of course, the author has to remember that the agent is also busy and has other clients who require attention and cosseting. Although the right to receive a full service from the agent plainly exists, it is sensible not to overstep the mark to the point of destroying the friendship which is so valuable a part of the relationship.

Friendly the author and the agent may be, but it must not be forgotten that their relationship is still essentially a business one. This is often underlined nowadays by the signing of a contract between author and agent. Not all agents use formal agreements, but in the absence of such a document the author can look for not only an oral discussion and, one hopes, a meeting of minds on all the expectations on both sides, but also a letter from the agent confirming the various points. If you are just beginning to work with an agent, and no agreement or letter has been offered, you should certainly ask for something in writing. You would then send the agent a written acceptance of the details which have been set out (and such correspondence will, of course, have the legal status of a more formal document).

An agent's contract

Most agents are honest, and there is little reason to fear that an agreement which an agent offers you will contain anything unfair or to your disadvantage, but there are one or two matters concerning which you should be aware of your rights.

Firstly, the contract should spell out all the percentages that the agent will take on various kinds of earnings (for example, as already suggested, a different rate from that applying to British royalties is likely to be levied on payments for USA or translation rights). The only exception to this rule should be if the agent wishes, for some special reason, to say that the percentage on a certain kind of income will be mutually agreed at a later date. It is not possible to give complete guidance on what terms are normal – agents vary in their charges – but if you are a member of the Society of Authors or the Writers' Guild you could ask their advice. Any member of the Association of Authors' Agents (indicated by an asterisk in *Writers' and Artists' Yearbook*) can be relied on not to charge unreasonably.

Secondly, the contract should specify any additional charges that the agent is entitled to make. Although a few agents insist on a reading fee from authors who are not already their clients, it is not normal for any other charge to be made until the agent has succeeded in placing the book with a publisher, apart perhaps from the cost of photocopying your typescript so that the agent is not limited to just one copy, and postage charges on sending copies abroad to foreign agents who might be able to interest publishers in their countries in taking the book for translation. After publication, the agent will probably wish to charge for copies of the book purchased from the publisher in order to send them to other possible rights buyers. It is not normal for an author to pay an annual retainer or any fee other than the agent's rake-off on the author's earnings.

The main point is that the author should be fully aware of the agent's charges and therefore should never be surprised either by the percentages taken, whatever the source of the money which the author has earned, or by any expenses which the agent wants to pass on. All these points must be clarified in the agreement or correspondence.

Thirdly, the contract should make clear whether it is intended that the agent should handle all the author's work, or only a part of it. The agent may be concerned, for instance, only with the author's books, and any journalism or short story writing or radio or television appearances which the author arranges will not be within the agent's remit – unless perhaps the agent has actually obtained a particular commission, in which case the agency would probably consider it justifiable to take a part of the money (and the author may well agree). Many agents are not in fact very interested in handling what might be called casual or minor work, such as the odd piece of freelance journalism, or anything similar for which, unless the author has a considerable reputation, the fee received is unlikely to be substantial enough for the agent to feel that his or her share is worth the hassle involved in handling the transaction.

Fourthly, there may be a need to clarify which subsidiary rights the agent will give to the publisher to control, and which the agent will retain. Book publishers normally expect to have at least volume rights (generally accepted as covering hardcover, paperback and bookclub publication), second serial rights and anthology or quotation rights. The agent will usually retain all other rights and attempt to sell them on behalf of the author. Sometimes, however, special circumstances arise, and the agent may agree to grant the publisher various extra rights, or it may be suggested, for instance, that the paperback rights should be handled by the agent rather than by the hardcover publisher (probably because the agent believes it possible to get a better deal that way). Although any such unusual arrangements of this sort can be worked out on a book by book basis, if they are to be permanent they should probably be agreed in advance between author and agent and included in the contract between them. As with all other matters, although it is important to listen carefully to the agent's advice (and most of them have a fair idea of what they are talking about) the author should be the final arbiter, and should not agree to any points which seem to be unreasonable.

One of the causes of occasional friction between authors and agents is that agents expect to stick quite rigidly to the arrange-ment that they will take their percentage on everything that the author produces (or everything within the limitations laid down – such as books only) even if the works concerned have been sold to a publisher (or film producer or whoever it may be) directly by the author without any involvement whatsoever of the agent. The agent's argument is that although he or she may not have been involved in the selling, the author will expect all the normal subsequent functions of an agent to be carried out, such as checking the contract, chasing the publisher, checking royalty statements, etc. . . Of course, you have the right to manufacture your own successes by direct contact with publishers or by any other means, even if your agent is not directly involved, but you should always keep the agent informed of what is happening, not only because your efforts may conflict with what he or she is doing, but also because it might turn out that good advice from the agent at an early stage might prevent you from committing yourself to a deal which would not be the wisest course for you. And if you really resent having to pay the agent's percentage, then you should probably break off the relationship and thenceforth handle everything yourself.

Finally, some statement of either party's right to terminate the arrangement should be included. An agency which takes on a client normally expects the arrangement to cover all the author's work from that point on, or at least, as already mentioned, in an agreed field, such as all books, or all fiction. The author may change publishers frequently, or have a number of publishers for various kinds of books, but can expect to remain with the same agency for all his or her work, and this stability is often greatly valued. However, it is the author's absolute right, if there is some reason for not wanting to stay wedded to a particular agency, to leave the firm at any point in time. If, therefore, you are signing up with an agency and the contract states that you agree to allow that agency to handle all your work 'irrevocably', strike out that phrase – no author should be irrevocably committed to an agent, any more than you would irrevocably commit yourself to buying your shoes in the same shop, or sticking to the same make of car.

Although you are free to leave your agent at any time and for any reason, there is a convention, often reflected in the agreement that an agent asks authors to sign, that the agent retains the right, even after you have both parted company, to take the normal agreed percentages from earnings of any books of yours which the agency has handled to the point of contracts being signed prior to your leaving the firm. Your new agent, if you have one, will therefore be involved only with the existing work for which no contract has been signed, and for any other work which you produce after joining him or her. Occasionally, an agent will agree to pass over his or her interest in a former client's work to a different agent, but it depends very much on circumstances, on the goodwill of the former agent, and, perhaps, on the value of the properties in question.

7
The publisher's rights

The author/publisher relationship

In the publication of a book, the publisher and the author are partners. The publisher would have nothing to publish if it weren't for the author, and the author would not usually have either the ability to produce and sell copies of his or her work, or in many cases sufficient available funds to do so. Each is dependent on the other. But for at least a couple of centuries, if it has been a partnership at all, it has been a very unequal one, in which the publisher has been totally dominant. The relationship has improved somewhat, from the author's point of view, over the last twenty years or so, but until quite recently there were still many publishers who felt that authors were an unfortunately necessary evil, that they should be seen and not heard, and that they were a stupid, ungrateful, demanding, vain, capricious kind of sub-stratum of the human race.

The attitude may have changed to some extent – with some enlightened publishers it has, indeed, been transformed – but even a medium-sized publishing house will receive something like a thousand submissions a year out of which to select the thirty or forty that will be published, and that fact means that the publisher is very firmly in a buyer's market. It's easy to be arrogant in that situation. And while all authors may not be stupid, vain or capricious, most of them are rather demanding and a bit ungrateful – how could they fail to be when they love their books more than anyone else ever could and are inevitably disappointed when they don't sell as well as they think they should?

The Minimum Terms Agreement

Although publishers may continue to think of themselves as in control because they are in a buyer's market, and may feel in their heart of hearts that Sir Frederick Macmillan was right to say that 'publishing would be fun, if it weren't for authors', things aren't quite the same as they used to be, and if one factor is primarily responsible for the fairly recent change of attitude it is the advent of the Minimum Terms Agreement.

The idea of the MTA originated with the Writers' Guild of Great Britain, growing out of the general perception of the times that individuals mattered and that no one should be financially exploited or deprived of the dignity of their labour. Authors have always been poorly paid (and still are – an average novel will probably take a year to write, and the author will be lucky to earn more than £1000 from it, which, it must be admitted, is considerably less as an annual income than an unskilled labourer would expect). And the buyer's market syndrome meant that for years publishers were all too ready to say, 'You're lucky to be published at all, so shut up, and don't grumble.'

This did not apply, of course, to established and prolific authors, especially those in the bestseller class, who would be given excellent terms and generally kowtowed to. That is neither surprising nor even unfair – stars always get star treatment. But the majority were not so lucky, and one of the problems for them was that the contracts were always drawn up by the publishers and even agents could rarely make much of a dent in what were known as 'standard trade practices'. Publisher-oriented agreements were not only ungenerous financially, but left the publisher in total control of all aspects of publication, and although the author was allowed to see proofs and to be paid any moneys due, there was always an unspoken suggestion that these were concessions made at the kind publisher's discretion, rather than anything which could be regarded as real, solid rights.

The Society of Authors joined with the Writers' Guild to produce in 1980 a document which they called a Minimum Terms Agreement. It was intended to be signed by the Society and the Guild on one side and the Publishers Association on the other, and it laid down terms, which it was hoped all publishers would incorporate, and even improve upon, in the agreements that they signed with individual authors who were members of either the Society or the Guild. The Publishers Association refused to sign the document, on the grounds that they were not constituted to commit all their members in that way, being no more than a consultative body. But although the PA would not even go so far as to commend the MTA, it was spurred to draw up a Code of Conduct for its members. This, while a somewhat wishy-washy affair which did not go very far towards meeting the principles embodied in the MTA, was at least an indication of some awareness that authors were seriously unhappy with the existing state of affairs.

The Society of Authors and the Writers' Guild then decided to approach publishing houses one by one to persuade them to sign the MTA, which they were prepared to vary in some details to suit the requirements of the publisher concerned, as long as the basic principles remained. Fifteen years on from the MTA's first appearance only eleven publishers (and there are probably well over three hundred in Britain) have signed, each agreement differing in certain respects from the others. The eleven signatories are all major houses, but that may still sound like a disaster. In fact the MTA has been a triumph for British authors.

First of all, although the Society and the Guild naturally saw the MTA as something which would benefit their members rather than those authors who did not belong to either organisation, most of the publishers who have signed up tend to offer its terms, or better, to all their authors. More importantly, without necessarily becoming signatories, almost all publishing houses have been affected by the MTA and have adopted many of its principles – indeed, many of those who have refused to sign have done so not because they are opposed to its terms, but because they claim already to be treating their authors at least as well as the MTA requires, while yet others say that their reason for not signing is not an objection to the terms, which they say they regularly offer or improve on, but the fact that each author and each book is so different that standard terms cannot and should not be laid down. And even those few houses which have not shifted from their pre-MTA dinosaur ways are at least conscious of the changes that have come about, are not surprised when their authors ask for the concessions which others give as a matter of course, and may sometimes yield on this or that point. Authors can certainly argue from a much stronger position than they could before the MTA was drawn up.

It has to be said that, for practical reasons, the MTA does not usually apply to books in which illustrations take up 40% or more of the space (which means the exclusion of many children's books), to specialist works on the visual arts in which illustrations fill 25% or more of the space, to books involving three or more participants in the royalties, or to technical books, manuals and reference books. However, even for these excluded categories, terms in general have tended to improve.

The thrust of the MTA is twofold. It is not merely concerned with financial matters, although it does lay down standards for the size of the advance (based on a prediction of the print quantity and retail price), the royalties on sales of various types (including the sales figures after which the royalty should increase), and the split between the publisher and the author of moneys from the sale of subsidiary rights (including US and translation rights). But it also addresses the relationship between the author and the publisher and the need to recognise that the author has a right to know what is happening with his or her book, a right to be kept informed, to be consulted about the way the book is published and publicised and sold, to have the opportunity to approve certain matters, such as the sale of subsidiary rights, before they can go ahead, and in general to be treated fairly as a partner in the enterprise. To a considerable extent the publisher's power over most aspects of publication remains in place (a point which will be discussed on more than one occasion later in this chapter and the next), but the MTA sets out to change basic attitudes radically, so that authors should no longer feel like second-class citizens.

Perhaps the most controversial part of the MTA is the suggestion that authors should give publishers a limited licence period in which to handle their books instead of licensing them for the entire period of copyright, which has been the convention in the past. This, and many other aspects of the MTA will be explored in the discussion of publishers' and authors' rights which follow in this and the next chapter, while any reader who wants to study an MTA and to go into the subject more deeply will find further material in two of my own books, *An Author's Guide to Publishing* and *Understanding Publishers' Contracts*. Additionally, the Society of Authors and the Writers' Guild will supply copies of the MTA, on request, to their members.

What the publisher expects

Any publisher's agreement, whether influenced by the MTA or not, will naturally place a number of obligations on the author, and the publisher has the right to expect the author to carry them out. However, it is always possible for an author to discuss any matters which seem unfair, and often to persuade the publisher to accept a different viewpoint. Most publishers are reasonable people if treated kindly, and since they are fond of saying that every book is different, they may readily accept the concept that your book (and/or you, for that matter) is sufficiently different to merit exceptional treatment in some respect or other.

Further consideration will be given in the next chapter to the author's right to question and discuss details of the contract and of the whole publishing procedure. In the meantime, let us look at the publisher's expectations as shown in the agreement.

The grant of rights

After a Preamble which identifies the parties to the agreement and allows for its benefits to be transferred on the one hand to the author's executors, administrators and assigns, and on the other to the publisher's administrators, assigns or successors in business, the contract proper then usually opens with a grant of rights, in which the author licenses to the publisher certain of the rights in the book for the publisher's own use and grants him or her control of other rights which the publisher may then sub-license to others. The grant of rights will specify the areas in which the publisher may exploit the work (the whole world, perhaps, or possibly only certain listed territories), the period of the licence, whether all rights in the work, or only some, are to be handled by the publisher, and the exclusive or non-exclusive nature of such rights. Authors can grant these rights, of course, because, assuming that they have written the book, and that it is all their own work, they own it totally in all its aspects.

If the author signs the agreement, the publisher is entitled to be confident that the author is in fact the owner of all the rights which he or she licenses and that those rights are not encumbered in any way – in other words that the supposed author really is the author, or if not, that the copyright in the work has legitimately come into his or her possession, and that no rights now licensed to the publisher have previously been given to someone else in a licence which is still operative. All that may sound like a very elaborate and contorted approach to something which is really quite simple, but some authors do not always remember what they own and what they do not, what they have already licensed and what is still available. It is quite easy, for example, for a British author to grant a publisher exclusive rights in the Common Market (this usually means, in publishing terms, the right to sell copies of the publisher's edition of the book in most foreign-language countries of the world) as well as in the Commonwealth, and then to grant an American publisher exclusive US rights and, by accident or through careless- ness, non-exclusive Common Market rights. As well as avoiding any confusion of that sort, the publisher should be able to rely on the author to understand that if rights have been granted to the publisher they remain within the publisher's control; if, for instance, the publisher has been licensed to sell translation rights, the author must not – at least, not without the knowledge and approval of the publisher – try, himself or herself, to sell translation rights directly to a foreign publisher.

Delivery of the typescript

One of the major causes of trouble between authors and publishers at an early stage in the publication process is the delivery and quality of a commissioned book, as opposed to one which the author writes 'on spec', as it were, and submits to a publisher in its completed form. Since the latter has already been delivered and accepted by the time the agreement is drawn up, there is no need for a delivery clause.

The first problem with commissioned books may be that the author does not stick to the agreed delivery date. Except in the case of a topical book, or one which is due to be published in order to coincide with some special event (such as an anniversary, or Wimbledon, or the start of the Proms, or the British tour of a major international pop star), publishers are usually fairly phlegmatic about delivery delays, provided that the book is not more than a few weeks, or months, late. They are used to authors who take their time – and to those who have difficulties in the shape of illness or bereavement, to which they will usually be sympathetic. If the delay goes on too long, they may get edgy, and ultimately angry, but that is hardly surprising. In any case, if the author is going to be late, the publisher should be told as early as possible.

Of course, 'delivery of the typescript' should mean delivery of the *complete* typescript, and publishers are entitled to be less than pleased if the author sends in the bulk of the book but then keeps them waiting for revised text or text permissions or pix, or something of that sort. And in such cases the author cannot be suprised if publication of the book is delayed.

The second problem is that publishers are entitled to expect the author to deliver a book which will not differ in content or length from the way it was envisaged when it was commissioned, and which will include any illustrative material, of a suitably high standard for reproduction, as specified in the contract. It doesn't always happen. Of course, books sometimes demand to be altered, during the writing process, from the way in which they were originally conceived – more space, or less, may be required, new material may emerge, and, if it is fiction, the plot and the characters may develop and change – and publishers are not usually too bothered unless the alterations result in a book which is radically different from the way it was planned. Even minor variations may be a problem if the author was given very tight and detailed specifications (which may be the case if the book is to be one of a series) and has strayed from those strict guidelines. Again, however, it is only sensible for the author to let the publisher know in advance of how the book will differ from the original plan.

The third problem is the quality of the typescript. You might think, with some justice, that if the book is commissioned, the publisher should make certain before signing the contract that the author is capable of producing a satisfactory book. Nevertheless, authors are not always reliable, and many a publisher's hope of receiving a brilliant book has been dashed when a dull, or inaccurate, or careless typescript is delivered – or one which suffers from all those faults and more besides. Such disappointments are part of publishing life. It isn't always the author's fault, of course, but the publisher has the right at least to expect the author to have done his or her best and to be prepared to do further work on the book if necessary to improve it. The MTA includes in the clause regarding delivery of the typescript a requirement for the publisher to inform the author within thirty days of any changes required, giving full details of these. At this point, the author, perhaps believing that the publisher is asking for unnecessary alterations, or is just being cussed, may refuse to amend the script, in which case the publisher has the right to decide whether or not to go ahead with publication. If the verdict is against doing so, some arrangement will have to be made concerning the cancellation of the contract, and the possible payment of compensation to the author; if the author is clearly at fault, the return to the publisher of any advance payment already made may be demanded.

One of the things which an author must accept is that a publisher always has the right to decide not to publish a book, and can do so because the author refuses to amend it in some way, or because the expected market seems to have shrunk or disappeared altogether, or for a variety of other reasons. The publisher may even change his or her mind about a book which has already been accepted, and decide not to go ahead. The author is somewhat powerless in such situations. If the agreement meets normal standards, it may be possible to force the publisher to publish, but to do so will probably mean having recourse to a court action, and that is expensive and will do nothing to enhance the relationship between publisher and author. You can imagine with what enthusiasm a publisher would publish such a book – you could expect sub-standard production, a minuscule print order, no promotion or publicity, and the remaindering of the book at the earliest possible opportunity. On the other hand, as already suggested, when a publisher cancels the plans for publication of a book, the author may be entitled to financial compensation, especially if it can be shown that the book meets the criteria asked of it when the project was first discussed.

(For the sake of some would-be authors living in cloud-cuckoo-land it may be worth pointing out while on this subject that they do not have an unalienable right to be published. All authors have to find a publisher who actually *wants* to bring the work out, and if they fail in that quest the only alternatives are to self-publish or to forget the whole idea. Publishers are free agents.)

The warranty

Publishing contracts normally carry a clause in which the author warrants to the publisher that the book concerned is his or her original work, that he or she is free to make the agreement with the publisher, that the facts in the book are true, and that it contains no libellous, obscene or injurious matter. The clause goes on to say that the author will indemnify the publisher against any expenses and loss resulting from a breach of the warranty.

In other words, the author guarantees not to have plagiarised someone else's book, or any part of it, that the rights in it (or at least any part of them covered by the publisher's contract) have not been previously sold to another party, and that the book contains neither any falsehoods or libels nor anything which could damage any reader (such as a recipe for a mushroom omelette made with *amanita phalloides*). If someone else's copyright material is being used, the author guarantees that permission has been or will be obtained.

The publisher has an absolute right to be able to rely on the warranty, and no author should ever sign a contract containing such a clause if there is any reason not to do so with a completely clear conscience. Publishers are always very sensitive on this matter, because breach of the warranty can lead not only to an expensive legal action and heavy damages, but to the withdrawal of the book, and consequent loss of all their production and other costs and their hoped-for profit. And however willing the repentant author may be to compensate the publisher in accordance with the terms of the contract, few authors have the means to settle the substantial sums which may be involved.

But why should it be the author's responsibility to make these warranties? Should the publisher not be the one to decide whether something in the book is unlawful? In fact, most publishers will spot anything obviously dangerous in a typescript, and many of them are willing to send a book to a libel lawyer for an expert opinion. As a result of what they themselves discover, or which is brought to their attention by a lawyer, they may ask the author to amend the material. If the author refuses to do so, the publisher would be justified in cancelling the contract, and demanding the return of any moneys paid. But the problem is that much unlawful material is not immediately obvious to the publisher or even to an expert – plagiarism, for instance, may be impossible to detect until the plagiarised author reads the published work, and since publishers are not necessarily expert in the field of specialised books, something which might be injurious to the reader could easily escape detection.

You may still not be entirely convinced, and may think that, after all, publishers are wealthy and can afford to take risks over things like libel. In fact, they *are* sometimes willing to take risks, if they think there is good reason for doing so. But they must know what they are letting themselves in for. So if your book contains anything which you think might be in any way unacceptable, tell the publisher about it frankly and fully. Then, if it is decided to ignore any potential danger, it will no longer be your sole responsibility. The one exception to this advice nowadays is the matter of obscene material; since almost anything goes, the publisher should be perfectly capable of picking out anything in this area which is so outrageous as to engage the professional attention of the Director of Public Prosecutions.

The licence

The publisher will expect to have the right to publish the book for a stated licence period. In the past the licence was usually for the period of copyright, which is to say that it would be in effect from the time the contract was signed until fifty years after the author's death. It would, of course, lapse if the agreement were rescinded at an earlier date than that, and most publishers would spell out in the contract the circumstances under which the rights would revert to the author. That is reasonable enough for a book which has a comparatively short selling life, but the MTA suggests that this arrangement is unfair on any authors whose books remain steadily in print over a long period, and it proposes that the licence period should be limited to a period of twenty years, after which a new agreement would have to be negotiated. It also allows, while the original contract would still be in force, for specific terms in it to be revised after a period of ten years.

Not surprisingly, most publishers dislike these proposals, and not all of those who have signed the MTA have accepted the clause which contains them. However, the Society of Authors and the Writers' Guild point out that (a) twenty years are a reasonable length of time, (b) the original contract may have incorporated terms which, however fair they were at the time, are now inadequate because of the status of the author and the book, and because of all kinds of developments in publishing and allied trades (this is obviously why the possibility of reviewing the terms after a ten-year period is suggested), (c) there may be many reasons why the author no longer wishes to be tied to the publisher in question (perhaps because all his or her other books have been published by a different house, perhaps because the book's original editor has left and the author no longer feels that there is a happy relationship, perhaps because, despite the book's steady sales, the author has never felt that the publisher did a good job – in fact, for all kinds of reasons), and (d) a publisher who has really done well for an author need rarely fear that the author will refuse to negotiate a new contract on reasonable terms. There is also the argument which says that since hardcover publishers normally use limited licence periods when they sub-license various rights, the principle should extend to the original agreement.

At the time of writing, few first-time authors are likely to be offered any shorter period than the full term of copyright, but the limited period will undoubtedly become standard procedure in due course.

The manner of publication

Most people believe that they are experts at their own jobs. Publishers are certainly convinced that they know more than any author about how to produce, package and sell a book successfully, and that includes knowing when to publish it and how to promote and publicise it. Although they are often ready nowadays to concede that the author should be kept informed of their plans, should be allowed a sight of the jacket and the blurb, should be consulted about where review copies should be sent, and so on, most of them still insist that the final decision in all these matters must be theirs.

This is not really surprising. After all, publishers do know a great deal about their business, especially if they are old-established firms; there's usually quite a lot of expertise in the newer firms too, because most of them are started up by people who have learnt their skills in other companies, and so bring a great deal of experience to their own business. As I write this I can hear the cynical laughter of many authors – and not only the disgruntled ones – who would maintain that publishers rarely seem to know a great deal about what they do, flying by the seat of their pants, as it were, and often making a hash of it. Two things have to be remembered, however: the first is that publishing is an extremely complex business, in which, because every book and every author are different, nothing is certain except that the whole thing is an enormous gamble; and the second is that almost all authors are less than fully informed about the problems of the business and are nearly always disappointed with their sales, so they are not the most reliable of critics.

There is also the little matter of finance. It is the publishers who pay for everything, and therefore it is not surprising that they want the final say in the manner of publication. The margin of profit on most books is minimal (bestsellers are, of course, different in this respect, as in many others), so to print more copies than will be sold can wipe out all the slender earnings; a slightly more lavish style of production than usual will mean that the retail price of the book has to go up, and that may have a terrible effect on sales; a rejected jacket design, quite apart from the cost of preparing a new one, may delay publication, which can sometimes have an adverse effect on the sales of the book, quite apart from the fact that the publisher has to wait longer before beginning to recoup the moneys already spent on the book (and, of course, like most businesses, publishing has a permanent cash flow problem, and runs largely on costly borrowed money). Problems of this kind – and there are many more – mean that the publisher wants as little interference from outsiders as possible in coping with them.

The publisher will always therefore insist on deciding on the format of the book, unless perhaps it is highly illustrated or unusual in some way – like a pop-up book, for instance – when the author's ideas on the shape and size of the book may prevail. I should make it clear that my definition of 'format' includes not only the size of the book, but the layout and the selected typeface and paper and type of binding.

The publisher is also very unlikely to take much notice of the author's views on the retail price, the print quantity and the publication date of the book.

Retail prices are dictated not only by the production costs (obviously, the bigger or more elaborate the book, and the more generously colour is used – colour printing is costly – the more expensive it will be) and by size of the print run (the more copies you print, the cheaper each is to produce), but by a consideration of what the market will bear. A high price for a book which is aimed at a specialist market will usually not put off the buyers, provided of course that the contents are of a really good standard.

The print quantity will be decided largely by the sales department, which will base its recommendations firstly on past experience, both general and specific in respect of the author's previous books (if any), secondly on the reports of the sales team who have been talking to booksellers and wholesalers about the book, and thirdly on a modicum of hunch. Naturally, if there is some special outside influence – a film or television tie-in, perhaps, or the promise of particular publicity – this will be taken into consideration.

What about the editors, you may ask – don't they have any influence on the quantity printed? Occasionally. Sales personnel are used to being told by editors that this book is brilliant, and that that book fills a long-felt want, and that the other book is destined to become the standard work on the subject. They have heard it all before, and their response may be a tidge cynical. But an editor's genuine excitement and enthusiasm can sometimes prove catching, so that the sales department is inspired to begin talking of increasing the proposed print quantity, instead of cutting it back. It doesn't always happen, of course, however excited and enthusiastic the editor may be. Like most things in publishing, it's all pretty unpredictable.

Most publishers get the print quantity wrong, either producing a few hundred too few, or a few thousand too many. There's no certain advice available, and no one else would do any better. It's a gambling business. The only time that an author is likely to have much effect on the print quantity is if he or she can persuade some third party, such as a club or society, to buy a substantial quantity (which probably means four figures) of the book for distribution or sale to the members.

The publication date also depends on a great many factors. The publisher will decide which are likely to be the most successful books on the list – a selection which is made quite dispassionately. (It may be worth taking this opportunity, while talking of the publisher's ability to consider the books on the list without allowing too much influence to personal feelings, to point out that you don't have to 'know someone' in order to get published; publishers aren't in the habit of publishing books because the authors are personal friends, or for any other reason than that they think the book is both good and saleable – or perhaps one should say both saleable and good.) The selection is also made pragmatically, for publishers usually know which of their geese are true swans, and the unexpected runaway success is a rarity. Many of the books which the publisher most favours will be scheduled for September or October, which are the prime months for Christmas sales (bookselling is very much a seasonal trade, with the last quarter of the year producing well over half the annual sales), and these will include not only fiction by bestselling authors, but popular general non-fiction, sports books, cookbooks, humour, and anything else which may appeal to the gift market. However, some good titles must be kept to be spread out over the quieter months. Some books are themselves seasonal or are tied to anniversaries, and educational books are usually published in the Spring, which allows teachers to decide on purchases for the next school year before the end of the summer term. And then there are the rest – the large numbers of books which do not have the stature to demand publication for the Christmas market and which have no 'natural' date attached to them. And for these the publisher has to make decisions which depend partly on what other books are on the publication schedule - most general publishers, whose lists embrace a large variety of books, try to keep some sort of balance in their monthly schedules – and partly on the achievements of the editorial, art and production departments - some books, because of various complications, have a much longer gestation period than others. On the whole, publishers want to bring their books out quickly, because only then can they start to get their investment back, but they are sometimes frustrated by the sort of gremlins that can get into the complex system and cause production delays.

Decisions on these aspects of the manner of publication – format, retail price, print quantity and publication date – are those which publishers feel they have an absolute right to make. The author may find that some publishers show a little more willingness to bend on such matters as the jacket and the blurb. Not so very many years ago it would have been almost unthinkable for a publisher to ask any but a bestselling author for his or her opinion of the proposed jacket design. Publishers believed that if authors were consulted, they were likely to ask for impossibly expensive illustrations, and would be generally difficult. And what did they know about it anyway? One of the results of the MTA is that many publishers nowadays are prepared to discuss the jacket with the author at an early stage, and will show him or her a rough design or even the finished artwork, partly in the hope of pleasing the author, but also giving an opportunity for an indication of great unhappiness, should that be the feeling. But if the author is critical of the design, the publisher is more likely to listen if the comments are made on factual rather than on artistic grounds – so notice might be taken if you were to point out in respect of the jacket on a historical novel that the period of the clothes depicted was entirely wrong, but a comment to the effect that the colours used in the illustration were not among your favourites would probably be ignored. On the whole, however, publishers still like to have the final right to go ahead even if the author is supremely unhappy with the jacket design.

Blurbs are rather different. Long before the MTA brought about a more liberal attitude, publishers frequently asked their authors to supply blurbs for their books – which was only sensible, seeing that the authors knew better than anyone else what the book was about. They then usually tarted the author's words up to a greater or lesser extent, especially adding in the bits about 'fills a long-felt want' or 'written with great sensitivity' or 'this brilliant study' which the modest author had baulked at putting on paper. But the results of their tinkering would probably not be seen by the author until the finished copies of the book arrived, and of course that was entirely so in the case of those books for which the publisher wrote the blurb without obtaining any contribution from the author. The same sort of thing still goes on, but publishers are much more ready than in the past to show the author the blurb and to allow him or her to ask for changes or to submit substitute material. It is comparatively easy and cheap to alter the wording of a blurb at proof stage or earlier; changing a jacket design is a much more frightening business (at least, it is to publishers).

Reprints

Authors are often aggrieved when publishers refuse to reprint their book when it has sold out. But the publisher is within his or her rights in refusing to do so. There is one recourse for the author (which we shall come to in the next chapter), but it has to be understood that publishers are as eager as anyone else to reprint if they believe that the demand for the book justifies it. And there's the rub. Although the author knows dozens of people who want to buy the book, and is sure that if only it were available, dozens more would flock to the bookshops in search of it, and hasn't the publisher forgotten that this is the eighty-fifth anniversary of whatever the book is about, which would surely boost the sales? despite all this, the publisher may not be able to see how a sufficient quantity is going to be sold to justify a reprint.

Reprints ought to be considerably cheaper to produce than the original edition – the publisher has already paid many of the initial costs, such as the typesetting of book, the preparation of the jacket, and so on – but start-up costs for a reprint, despite modern technology (which has speeded the process remarkably) are still high enough to mean that the publisher will have to order a substantial quantity to be produced if the reprint is to be economic. In inflationary times, the costs are more likely to force an increase in the retail price, rather than allow it to continue at the old level with a better profit margin.

The author may be quite right in saying that dozens of people would like to buy the book, but the publisher will have to look, not for dozens, but for several hundred new buyers. And in any case, the dozens may turn out to be a single half-dozen when you get down to the truth of the matter. As for those others who would buy the book if it were available, the publisher has some justification for scepticism – if people have been asking for it in shops and going away empty-handed, the publisher will undoubtedly have heard of it. So, if a reprint is put in hand, where is it going to be sold? The public libraries won't want any more copies, and bookshops, faced with seventy thousand new books appearing every year, prefer to stock something new, rather than a book which has already had its turn.

These are the kind of reasons why publishers often refuse, to the author's dismay, to reprint a book. And, of course, they don't do so without having watched the rate of orders for it which they have continued to receive since it became unavailable, or without weighing reports from their sales staff, or without considering any factors (such as that eighty-fifth anniversary) which might boost the sales – or those which might have the opposite effect (such as an increase in the retail price, or perhaps the publication of a strongly competitive volume).

It's a cruel world, and a great many authors have to face the unpalatable fact that thousands of the books which are published every year are dead within six months or less of their publication, and although they can occasionally be resuscitated, it takes pretty unusual circumstances for that to be possible. That short life is certainly true of a high proportion of the fiction published, while in non-fiction a book has the best chance of living to a ripe old age if it can be regarded as the standard work on its subject, which usually means that it is essentially, or to a considerable degree, educational or instructive. If sufficient demand is there, it will be a very unusual publisher who refuses to reprint – despite the high start-up costs already mentioned, a successful reprint is the jam on the publisher's bread and butter – but, as with the initial publication, a substantial amount of the firm's money will be at risk, and he or she will certainly insist on having the sole right to make the decision.

Revised editions

Much the same facts apply to revised editions as to reprints, but there are also the balancing factors that, on the one hand, a substantially new edition will clearly cost more than a straight reprint, while, on the other, it may be easier to persuade the book-sellers to stock a book which has at least some pretence to be new.

Some books are expected to undergo annual revision – reference books which need to be updated regularly, such as *Writers' and Artists' Yearbook* (an indispensable tool of the writer's business for over eighty years) – and this will have been envisaged and no doubt agreed at the time of the first signing up of the book in question. Other non-fiction books will almost certainly have had to establish themselves in their particular field, possibly with several reprints having been put in hand over the years, before the publisher will consider the idea of a revised edition, although this may happen earlier if the material in the original version has become so out of date as to make the book useless or even ridiculous.

Publishers will probably listen fairly sympathetically to a writer who asks that a revised edition should be issued, in place of another straightforward reprint of the original edition, but whatever the reasons and justifications for the request, it will be the publisher who makes the final decision, having the sole right to do so.

Subsidiary rights

At contract stage the publisher will in most cases have been given a licence allowing not only the production of his or her hardcover and/or paperback editions of the book in question, but also the sub-licensing of third parties in a number of different ways – the company may control the sale to others of subsidiary and other rights, including paperback, bookclub, US, translation, first and second serial, anthology, etc.

These subsidiary rights are of great importance to publishers, most of whom, if they are of any size, have a subsidiary rights department as an important, and indeed, essential part of their organisation. When they sell the subsidiary rights they share the proceeds with the author (the Minimum Terms Agreement, of which examples can be found in my books, *An Author's Guide to Publishing* and *Understanding Publishers' Contracts*, gives examples of fair splits), and the publisher is often dependent on his rake-off from the sale of these rights to make publication of the book possible and profitable and, indeed, for the survival of his business. This does not apply to every book, but is certainly true of fiction by any but a bestselling author, and also of many non-fiction books aimed at a general, rather than a specialist, market.

In the past, publishers had the right to make deals for any of the subsidiary rights which they controlled with any sub-licensees they liked without consulting the author. The assumption was that the author would be as pleased to hear that extra money would be forthcoming as the publisher was to have his costs subsidised.

A certain amount of change has been brought about in this matter, partly by the MTA and partly by pressure resulting from some best-selling authors discovering angrily that the paperback rights in their books had been taken away without their knowledge from existing sub-licensees so that the publisher who controlled the rights could bring them out under his or her own paperback imprint. The change is not of huge significance, but many publishers will now agree to consult their authors before any subsidiary rights sale has been finalised and ask for their approval. In some cases, an agreement will go beyond that point and lay it down that the deal cannot go ahead at all if the author disapproves.

Like many other points, this seems a reasonable enough idea, so why is it that publishers often resist it? The main reason is that far more hardcover publishers own a paperback imprint nowadays than used to be the case, and they want the right to put their hard-cover books into their own paperback concern without having to convince anyone that it is a wise move. Apart from that, it comes back, I think, to the question of the publisher's belief in his or her own expertise, coupled with a fear that this or that author might refuse to give approval of a deal for reasons which were inadequate and perverse or which resulted from ignorance of the business. If an offer for a sub-licence from, say, a paperback house, is rejected, it may not be possible to find another taker for the book. And if the author's reason for rejection is that the offer isn't a very good one, then it is worth remembering that the publisher needs the money just as badly, and, knowing the market, would go elsewhere if it seemed likely that a better deal could be achieved. Don't be surprised therefore if you come across publishers who insist that, once an author has licensed them to control certain rights, they should be left to handle them as they think fit, and that this is a right to which they are entitled for taking the book on in the first place.

Returns

Almost all general books are distributed to bookshops on a sale or return basis (except for those actually ordered by customers), which means that the bookseller is guaranteed against the loss which might be sustained as a result of over-ordering by the ability to return unsold copies for credit. If this system did not exist, the stock in bookshops would be largely limited to known bestsellers and such bread-and- butter lines as dictionaries, Bibles and the works of W. Shakespeare. The trouble is that even if the author, while not perhaps in the bestseller class, can be considered to be 'established', there is never any certainty about how his or her latest book will sell. The problem is at its most acute in the case of novels, but it also applies to almost all genres except those aimed at very specialist markets. Although if they are wise they do not over-sell, just as the bookseller should have enough sense not to over-order too hugely, publishers have to do everything they can to persuade booksellers to take their books – if they are not in the shops, there is little hope of sales to the public – even if there is a risk of some of them being returned later, in which case it is quite likely that they will eventually have to be remaindered (see below) or destroyed. And if they have been damaged they will certainly have to be pulped.

The main difficulty as far as the publisher's dealings with the author are concerned is that, since the unsold books may not be returned until several months after they were originally delivered to the shops, the publisher may be in the position of paying the author royalties on books which have not in fact been finally sold.

You might think that this situation poses a minor problem only, since all the publisher has to do is to reclaim the over-payment from the author. It sounds fine in theory; in practice, it just doesn't work, because publishers find it impossible in most cases to get money back from their authors (as a class, authors tend not to be particularly flush, and very often have spent the royalties as soon as they were received – or even before), and in any case, any attempt to do so is almost certain to cause bad feeling.

From the publisher's point of view, the answer would be not to pay any royalties at all until the sales were known to be positively firm, but that would be quite unacceptable to authors. The solution which most publishers therefore use is to insert a clause in their agreement giving them the right to make a reserve against returns. The publisher then has the right to withhold 'against returns' a given percentage (specified in the agreement) of the royalties apparently earned during the first royalty period after publication. The reserve is held for an agreed number of further royalty periods, after which it is fed back in, and if sales have exceeded returns the moneys due to the author are paid.

This is not unfair, provided that the percentages reserved are not excessive, and almost all publishers in almost all cases will see the reserve as a right which they will insist on exercising.

Remainders

As has already been said, it is almost impossible to guess accurately exactly the right number of copies of a book to print. If the book has been underprinted and there is a substantial demand for additional copies, especially if it is going to go on selling year after year, it doesn't matter very much whether the initial print quantity was right or not – the book can always be reprinted. The problem in fixing the wrong initial print figure for books which do not have a long, sustained shelf-life is either that a fairly small number of additional copies should have been printed (although there is insufficient demand to justify a reprint), or – and this is a far more frequent occurrence – a few hundred or even a few thousand too many copies have been produced. You may think that this is extremely bad management on the publisher's part, but any business which is equally unpredictable is likely to appear equally inefficiently run.

What can publishers do with their overstocks? Authors sometimes think that the books should be re-launched, advertised again, and in fact treated almost as though they were completely new titles. Unfortunately, this just doesn't work. Booksellers cannot be persuaded to re-order books which have ceased selling; as for advertising, except in the case of specialist books advertised in specialist magazines, it is simply not economically viable unless the publisher is prepared to spend a really large sum of money in order to get blanket coverage, and that will probably be done only to boost the sales of an already recognised bestseller. The books are doing no good sitting on the warehouse shelves – in fact it costs money to keep them there. There are only two courses of action available to the publisher – one is to destroy the surplus copies, and the other is to remainder them.

In the publishing world, 'remainder' is a verb as well as a noun. 'To remainder' means to sell off the balance (the remainder) of the edition to a 'remainder merchant' at a knock-down price, which is very often less than the production cost. The remainder merchant then puts the books on sale to the public at bargain prices. Sometimes, the publisher is unable to persuade any of the remainder merchants to take copies of a given book, perhaps because it is of too specialist a nature or has become completely out of date, or because the overstocks are too enormous, and in that case the books may have to be pulped. This is a course which pleases no one. If the books are destroyed the author naturally receives no royalties for them. What happens if they are remaindered? It is usual for contracts between authors and publishers to say that if remainders are sold by the publisher at a price per copy above the cost of manufacture, the author will receive a 10% royalty on the proceeds, but that if the remainder merchant's payment is less than the manufacturing cost, no royalty will be paid. Alas, remainders are almost invariably sold at less than the cost of manufacture, so the author gets nothing (but see p. 90).

The MTA states that books shall not be destroyed or remaindered until one year after first publication. This seems reasonable, although publishers sometimes feel that they should be allowed a shorter period in the case of books which have revealed themselves within a few weeks of publication to be total failures. The main point to be made, however, is that whenever the agreement allows the publisher to do so, he or she has an absolute right to make the decision to remainder or destroy the surplus copies.

Infringements

If a book's copyright or the exclusive licences given to a publisher in respect of it are infringed, the publisher will wish to take action against the offending party, and has the right to do so not only in the case of the licences, but also if the copyright is breached, even though the author may (and indeed should) own the copyright. The publisher will normally expect the author to join in any action to protect the rights, but if the author declines to do so (perhaps not thinking the matter important, or fearing an extremely expensive lawsuit, or being lost in the Amazon jungle and therefore not aware of the problem), then the publisher has the right to take action independently in the names of both the author and the publishing company.

Option

An option clause used always to form part of a publishing agreement. It guaranteed the publisher the right to publish the author's next book, and very often specified the terms of the contract. Although the option was probably regarded as of particular importance in the case of fiction, the clause was also normally included in the contracts for non-fiction books.

If you are a one-book author, that fact will not stop you from finding a publisher provided that your one book has the right kind of appeal; nevertheless, publishers generally are more interested in authors who can produce a number of publishable books, because the sales will build up as a succession of books appears and the author becomes known both to booksellers and to the book-buying public. Many bestselling authors have begun with modest sales and gradually increased their reputations so that eventually not only is each new book a bestseller, but the earlier, less successful titles can be reprinted. Publishers feel that their initial interest in their authors, the effort they put into launching them on the market, and the subsequent building up of their sales and reputations deserve the reward of a right to continue to publish those authors, and they cannot depend on this unless the agreement contains a firm option clause, because authors are fickle and easily tempted by offers from rival publishers.

The Society of Authors and the Writers' Guild, on the other hand, are strongly opposed to options in any form, and advise authors always to strike out any option clause which a publisher may insert in a contract. They believe that a publisher should *earn* the right to continue publishing an author, rather than to have it set in stone. However, recognising that publishers really do feel the need to have some kind of lien on their authors, the MTA includes a clause which says that the publisher may ask the author for first refusal on his or her next work. The author can decide not to comply, but if he or she does, the publisher must either make an offer for the book or reject it within three weeks (one of the other bones of contention in the past was that publishers took far too long to make up their minds about books submitted under an option clause).

8

The author's rights under a publisher's contract

YOUR BASIC RIGHTS

As has already been explained in the previous chapter, it is only comparatively recently, and especially as a result of the introduction of the Minimum Terms Agreement, that authors have begun to feel that publishers have moved some way towards treating them as partners, rather than as if they were Victorian children to be seen and not heard. However, even in the days when publishers appeared to look upon authors as second-class citizens, the author had certain basic rights.

The first right, naturally, was that of expecting that the publisher would adhere to the terms of the contract. Agreements are legal documents, and enforceable in a court of law, and the publisher therefore had to carry out the obligations which the agreement imposed. The same is still true today. These duties usually include the actual publication of the book, the protection of the author's copyright (unless, of course, the author has assigned it to the publisher), the payment of moneys due, and the unencumbered reversion of rights in certain circumstances. Authors may feel that they have rights on many other matters, but, despite the influence of the MTA, this is not always so. We shall look first at the rights which are undeniably given to the author, and shall consider subsequently those which depend on the publisher's willingness to make concessions.

The publisher's commitment to publication of the book

You would think that publishers, having signed an agreement to publish a certain book, would want to bring it out as soon as possible, especially if money in the form of an advance had been paid to the author. In most cases they do, and are reasonably prompt in publishing the books on their lists. But there are cases where the publication of this, that or the other book has been delayed for months or years, or even indefinitely, and for a variety of reasons, some of which may be valid, but others less so – such as not having enough money, or thinking that other books are more urgent, or having simply forgotten all about it.

The author should make sure when signing the contract that the publisher agrees to bring the book out within a specified time. Don't be satisfied with an assurance that the book will be published 'within a reasonable period' – that leaves the publisher free to decide what is 'reasonable', and his or her idea of that may not be the same as yours.

The publishing process for the average book takes about nine months from the date of acceptance to publication. Books are some-times rushed out much more quickly in order to cash in on some topical event, and others sometimes take very much longer because of their complexity (or possibly because of various disasters that happen during production). Although the ordinary book may take the standard nine months, it will not necessarily be published at the end of that period, because, as has already been explained, publishers choose the time of publication so as to give each book (and especially their bestsellers) the best possible chance of good sales, and at the same time so as to keep a balance in the list as a whole. An acceptable time-scale for the author of an average book to look for in the contract, therefore, is that publication shall take place within one year, or perhaps eighteen months, of delivery of the typescript. Eighteen months is just about the outside limit, unless, because of the nature of the book, its production is going to be a very lengthy business, or possibly because the publisher needs time to arrange a co-edition with one or more foreign publishing houses. If the publisher wants longer than eighteen months, the author should be given a satisfactory explanation for the delay.

It is worth noting that while the publisher has little means of redress against an author who fails to carry out the obligations which the agreement demands, and can only express displeasure and hope that the failing will be rectified, the author can often obtain tangible compensation if the publisher fails in his or her contractual duties. For instance, if the publisher delays the appear-ance of the book beyond the date set in the agreement, the author can often expect to receive that part of the advance due to be paid on publication on the date by which, according to the contract, publication should have taken place.

Cancellation of the contract

Occasionally (fortunately, not so frequently as was the case some few years ago), instead of merely delaying publication of a book, the publisher decides not to go ahead with it, and cancels the contract. The reasons for this may vary from lack of cash to a conviction that the book would be a total failure. Publishers go bust quite often, so the shortage of cash may be a very valid reason for cancellation if the firm happens to be in difficulties. And if the company is trying to trim its sails to the cold winds of a recession, sometimes a decision has to be made to go ahead with this book and to cancel that one, and if the feeling is that your book is not so likely to succeed as the other, you will be the one to suffer. Alternatively, it may be that the genre seems to have gone out of fashion, or that a rival publisher has just brought out a competitive volume which looks as though it will scoop the field, or it could be (and very often is) that the editor who persuaded the firm to take the book on has left the company, and there is now no one there who likes the book enough to fight for it. Publishing, despite all the talk of the cold hand of the accountant controlling everything, is still decided sometimes by personal enthusiasms, and an editor who is really fired up about a particular book can often persuade his or her colleagues, including those cold fish in the accounts department, that the book is one which just must be signed up; on the disappearance of that editor, the spur to all the other departments of the business can vanish too.

It is, of course, a bitter blow for any author to learn that his or her book is not after all to be published. Compensation should be paid, and should not only include any part of the advance still unpaid, but also an allowance for the royalties over and above the advance which the author could have expected the book to earn, and possibly some general damages too.

The fact that the publication of a book has been cancelled does not necessarily mean that it will not see the light of day. The author may be able to persuade a different publishing house to take it on. Some publishers say that if they cancel a book and pay compensation to the author, the latter should refund the money, or at least a part of it, if the book finds a home with another publisher. Although one can appreciate the publisher's point of view, unless this has been agreed in writing at the time of cancellation of the original contract, the author is not obliged to accept the suggestion. The outcome will depend on the degree of understanding of the publisher's problems which the author has, the way in which the cancellation was handled, and perhaps the author's need (or greed) for money.

Protection of copyright

It is the publisher's duty to protect the author's copyright, and it is in his or her own interest to do so. It is done, as has already been described, by printing a copyright notice in the book, giving the name of the copyright owner and the date of publication (and probably including the sign ©).

There is, however, an additional requirement in this country, which is that the publisher should supply copies of the book, free of charge, to the British Library, the Bodleian Library, the Library of Cambridge University, the National Library of Scotland, the National Library of Wales and the Library of Trinity College, Dublin. The law that copies of all published books should be supplied to these libraries was enshrined in the Copyright Act of 1911 as a prerequisite for the establishment of copyright. Although there is no mention of the requirement in the 1988 Act, and copyright exists internationally whether books have been distributed to these libraries or not, they still have a legal right to their freebies. Publishers resent having to give away these copies, especially if the book happens to be a very expensive one. But they have to do it.

As was made clear in the section on Moral Rights (see p. 33), although publishers will usually include in their books a notice setting out the author's right to be identified as the author of the work – the so-called Right of Paternity – they are not in fact under any obligation to do so unless the author requests the inclusion of such a notice, in which case they have no option but to comply.

The author may also reasonably expect the publisher to pursue any infringements of copyright. If any action is to be taken by the publisher in respect of infringement of the author's copyright and the publisher's licences, the author has a clear right to be consulted and to join the legal action if he or she is able to do so.

Proofs

The author has a right to see a proof copy of the work, and to make corrections before the book is printed. The agreement often specifies a maximum period of time for the correction of proofs and the author must obviously adhere to it. Even minor alterations to the proof are very expensive, and while the printer is responsible for the correction of printer's errors, you will have to pay for what might be called your 'second-thoughts' changes if their cost exceeds a certain percentage, usually stated in the contract, of the price the publisher pays for the whole book to be set up in type. Sometimes a large number of alterations at proof stage is essential, perhaps because last-minute additions and alterations will be needed so that the book will be as up-to-date as possible. If you foresee such a situation, talk to the publisher about it in advance, and it may be possible to find a solution to the problem of the high extra costs.

Free copies

The author may expect to be given free copies of his or her book on publication, the number of such copies being specified in the agreement. Traditionally, these free copies have been limited to six, but some publishers, realising perhaps that one of the cheapest ways of pleasing the author is to be a little more generous with the complimentaries, have increased the number to twelve. It should certainly be twelve, if not twenty, in the case of a mass-market paperback. Some publishers will also agree to present the author with at least one copy of any revised edition of the book. Of course, royalties are not payable on the author's free copies.

The clause of an agreement which deals with author's copies usually also carries wording to the effect that the author is entitled to buy further copies of the book at a trade discount. Many agreements do not specify what this discount will be, and such a wording as 'the author may purchase additional copies at best trade terms' is vague and may mean only the best terms that the publisher is willing to offer to an author, rather than referring to the high discounts that a large trade customer may receive. It is preferable to have the actual discount stated (the MTA suggests further that the terms may vary according to whether the author is paying cash or asking for the sales to be charged to his or her royalty account). Royalties are payable on the copies which the author purchases in exactly the same way as on other sales, and will be included in due course on the royalty statement.

The copies which an author buys are expected to be for personal use, and not for re-sale. This restriction is designed to protect booksellers, publishers preferring any additional sales that an author can achieve to go through trade outlets, because they like to support booksellers, and try to avoid antagonising them. However, special arrangements can usually be made for an author who can sell copies of his or her books to a particular market, such as a society or club, which could probably not be tapped in any other way, or for authors attending the increasingly widespread gatherings of members of writers' circles and similar groups, where books by those present are often on sale. Publishers will insist, however, that any such sales should be at the full retail price of the books.

The payment to the author of moneys due

One of the publisher's obligations towards the author is to pay promptly any moneys due. So if a part of the advance is to be paid on signature, or on delivery of the typescript or on publication, or at any alternative stated date, the author should be able to rely on receiving it on that date. But what do you do if your publisher is one of those (fortunately few) who are very lax in this respect? An agent, if you have one, will undoubtedly pursue the matter, and if you are a member of the Society of Authors or of the Writers' Guild, either of those organisations will take action on your behalf. It is much more difficult if you are on your own, especially since you may fear upsetting the publisher by making an issue of the late payment of the advance. Nevertheless, the publisher has an obligation towards you, and you have every right to protest if he or she fails to accept it. (If you are really in trouble in this respect, you might consider having recourse to the Small Claims Court.)

The same is true of royalties. Most publishers work on six-monthly royalty accounting periods, which is to say that they render accounts to their authors twice yearly, and pay any royalties or other earnings due at those times; some publishers, however, (mostly academic houses) send out their accounts only once a year. In my opinion, a royalty period of longer than six months is quite unfair. Authors' accounts are undoubtedly extremely complex, especially since the terms for almost every book differ in some respect or other, but with the modern technology of computers, it should be perfectly possible for all publishers to render accounts not merely every six months, but quarterly. Of course, for authors to think of being paid every three months is pie in the sky; publishers will argue that any such arrangement would involve them in extra costs (the stationery for the statements, the postage, and the additional bank charges, let alone the staff expenses) and that additionally it would increase their cash flow problems. Nevertheless, it may happen one day.

Whatever the royalty period may be, the author is entitled to expect prompt payment on the due date, which is usually three months after the end of every royalty period. That is something else which may one day change for the better. The three-month delay was totally understandable in the days when all the ledgers and the statements and cheques themselves had to be prepared by hand, especially in a large publishing house which might have to report on a thousand or more active titles. But is it reasonable when computers could probably turn out all the details, all the statements, and prepare all the cheques ready for signature in a matter of hours? No, it isn't, despite the fact that it would exacerbate the publisher's cash-flow problems to pay more rapidly. But any thought of change is again pie in the sky, and in the meantime authors simply have to accept that all is not perfect in this imperfect world, and that one of the imperfections is having to wait for your money.

One of the most important changes that has taken place in recent years (largely as a result of widespread acceptance of many of the principles of the MTA) is that many publishers now agree that if reasonably substantial sums of money – by which is meant £100 or more – are paid to them by sub-licensees, they will pass on the author's share of the earnings as soon as they receive the payment, instead of waiting for the next royalty period before handing it over, provided that the advance on the book in question has already been covered. If your publisher has signed an MTA, this method of accounting will be laid down in the agreement and will be your right; otherwise, if you get it, it will be a privilege, rather than something to which you are automatically entitled. It should be noted, however, that this applies mainly to advances and royalties paid under sub-licences; where publishers sell copies of their edition of a book to a sub-licensee (e.g. to a bookclub), the royalties on such sales will be treated like any other royalties under the main agreement for the book, and paid at the regular six-monthly times.

Finally, the author has every right to expect accuracy in the accounts. Alas, errors are far from unknown, and if you do not have an agent to do the job for you, you should check the royalty statements with great care to ensure that all the royalty rates and other percentages are correct. It is not that publishers set out to cheat the author – by and large, they must rank among the most honest of businessmen, despite the beliefs of some authors – but, as has already been mentioned, authors' accounts are enormously complex, and it is not surprising that those who enter the relevant figures into the computer should occasionally make mistakes. Most agreements give the author the right to examine the publisher's accounts in respect of a given book if the author believes that an inaccuracy may exist.

Public Lending Right

PLR and the moneys that may come from it belong by law to the author and to the author alone. An agent, if you have one, should not be involved in any way with PLR, and should certainly not take a percentage of it (unless you insist that he or she should deal with the registration of your titles and any matters arising therefrom – a chore which most agents resist taking on, saying that they have quite enough to do already – in which case you will have to pay for the work involved). So your publisher is not entitled to any share in your PLR, and, although most publishers now take this for granted, it does no harm to have a clause in the contract underlining the point.

Remainders

As has already been explained, it is the publisher's right to decide at some point in time that sales of a given book are so slow that it would be best to dispose of the remaining stock by remaindering or destroying it. However, the author does have the right to be informed that the book is to be remaindered or destroyed, and in the latter case, should be given any copies which he or she requires free of charge; if the book is to be remaindered, the author should be able to buy copies from the publisher at the price which has been negotiated with the remainder merchant.

It is a sad day when you are told that your book is to be remaindered. The one very small consolation is that, although as already explained you do not get any royalties on the remaindered copies, at least you should be able to buy a supply of the book very cheaply, to give away or to sell.

Not all publishers are scrupulous in remembering their obligation to inform the author of remaindering plans, so if you think that there is any likelihood of your publisher remaindering one of your books – the signs are there if the royalty statements show very slow sales – then it is worth reminding him or her that you will want the chance of buying copies at the remainder price.

Reversion of rights

Writers should always ensure that a publisher's agreement includes a clause setting out the circumstances under which the contract shall be terminated and all rights in the book shall revert to the author. Of course, this cannot happen if the author has assigned the copyright to the publisher (a course which, as has already been pointed out, is to be avoided if at all possible.)

There are three main circumstances in which termination of the contract may occur. The first is if the publisher goes into liquidation. This does not mean simply that the firm is taken over by another publishing house, as has become a frequent happening in the trade in recent years, because in such cases the new owner would expect to continue to sell the books on the list of the publisher which has been taken over. It applies instead when the publisher becomes bankrupt and ceases trading, and a receiver is appointed. In such events, the rights should revert to the author automatically, provided that the agreement states specifically that this will happen (try to ensure that it does). If it does not, the receiver will treat any books on the failed publisher's list, and the licences attached to them, as assets of the business, and the author may face many problems as a result.

The second possibility is the publisher's failure to comply with the terms of the agreement. In most cases when the contract is terminated for this reason the shortcoming is likely to be a serious one, and the publisher will probably have refused to put it right or even to explain the problem despite requests from the author to do so. In other words, some degree of unreasonableness on the part of the publisher is likely to have been evident. You wouldn't expect to ask for termination if the publisher were six months late in bringing the book out, especially if you were given a fairly acceptable explanation of the delay, but you would certainly have a case if the publication were delayed for several years and if the publisher refused to schedule the book or give you any valid reason for not doing so. Equally, you won't have much of a case for termination if all that you can claim is that your book has not sold as well as you hoped, or that the publisher has not used his or her 'best endeavours' to promote it ('best endeavours' is one of those weasel phrases which are often to be found in agreements – 'the publishers will use their best endeavours' to do this or that – which are virtually meaningless, since it is impossible for disputants to agree on even a commonsense meaning of the words, let alone a legal one); you need to be able to point to a quantifiable failure in clear breach of the contract.

The most frequent circumstance in which reversion takes place is when the book is out of print or has been remaindered. Publishers rarely refuse to allow the rights to revert if they can see no future for their own exploitation of the rights in the book in question. However, they will probably refuse to agree to termination if the book is still active in any form which they have sub-licensed to another party, and their right to do so is usually included in the original agreement. Alternatively, the publisher may allow the rights to revert on the understanding that he/she will continue to receive any income due from existing sub-licences until they expire.

Although, as I say, publishers are not in the habit of adopting a dog-in-the-manger attitude to books which seem to them to be dead, they don't volunteer to revert rights. After all, the book may suddenly become active again because of some unforeseeable outside influence (a film, or a major news item about the subject, for instance). So the author has first to write to the publisher asking for termination and reversion of rights on the appropriate grounds. If the book is out of print, it may be necessary to begin by giving the publisher formal notice that the book should be reprinted within a period which is laid down in the contract. Sometimes the publisher will reply promptly that a reprint is not justified and that the rights may therefore revert to the author forthwith, but in other cases the author may have to wait a short while for the publisher to make a decision.

Arbitration

One further right which is usually enshrined in agreements and which protects both author and publisher is the right to seek arbitration from an outside source if the two parties disagree. This is perhaps of particular interest to authors, who may otherwise feel that they will be at a considerable disadvantage in any dispute with a publishing house, simply because publishers have money and authors don't, publishers have expert legal advisers and authors don't, and publishers are many and authors are on their own.

It is usual for the agreement to specify that arbitration may be conducted by someone whom both parties to the dispute will accept as suitable, or in accordance with the Arbitration Act of 1950, which would mean recourse to an official arbitrator.

THE AUTHOR'S RIGHTS UNDER THE MINIMUM TERMS AGREEMENT

The MTA, as has already been explained, can be regarded as having two basic concepts: it is concerned both with the author's financial rewards and with the author's right to be consulted on many matters concerned with the production and sale of the book. Do remember as you read on that the MTA suggests *minimum* terms – if you can achieve more, do so.

The MTA does not lay down minimum cash sums which every author could expect to be paid. Because books are so varied in every way, and are liable to earn different sums of money depending on their price and sales in volume and other forms, there is no question of setting a minimum acceptable payment for an author's work in cash terms. What the MTA has striven to establish is a series of percentages which could be applied in various ways to all books in order to produce an acceptable share of the expected or hoped-for proceeds from its publication.

The amount of money that an author can earn from a book varies from almost nothing to a fortune. Fortunes are rare, and to earn them you have to be an established bestseller or to burst upon the publishing scene with a book which is exceptionally good of its kind, lends itself to publicity and promotion, can be serialised, paperbacked, bookclubbed, made into a film, and so on. Turn up with a book like that and you will certainly be flavour-of-the-month. But that sort of thing is a pipe dream for most authors, and the MTA has been mainly concerned with improving the lot of ordinary writers – the high fliers can look after themselves, or pay others to do so.

As for consultation, although it may take place very amicably, and the publisher has a duty to consider carefully any points which the author puts forward – indeed the whole process must be taken seriously, rather than becoming a merely cosmetic exercise – despite this, in the end the publisher will probably make the final decision on almost all the matters which may come under discussion.

It must also be borne in mind that even those publishers who have signed an MTA may wish to vary it in specific cases, on the same old basis that every book is different and so is every author. Any single clause in the contract may vary from one book to another, not excluding those in the MTA which do not appear to allow much latitude for change, such as the financial arrangements.

The advance

The MTA suggests that the author should be paid an advance based on his or her expected earnings from the proposed first printing of the book. The publisher is therefore called upon, at the time that the agreement is drawn up, firstly to decide what quantity of the book will be printed, secondly to assume a certain published retail price, and then to calculate, assuming that the entire printing is sold, what the author's earnings would be, taking into account the fact that the royalties per copy would vary according to whether the books were sold in the home market at full price, or in the export market, or in special deals at a discounted rate. The advance should then be calculated, the MTA states, at 65% of those earnings if the work is to be published only in hardcover or only in paperback, or at 55% if it is to appear in both formats from the one publisher.

This is less of a chore for the publisher than it may sound. Most publishers nowadays prepare estimates of expenditure and receipts for each book that they take on, and the procedure outlined in the previous paragraph approximates to the manner in which they often calculate the advance which they could offer the author.

On the other hand, the amount which they propose may be an enormous sum, suggested in the hope of luring a very desirable author to join the list, or because they expect to be able to recoup most if not all of it by lucrative deals with sub-licensees. Alternatively, they may offer as little as they think they can get away with, because the less money they have to pay out the less they will have to pay in interest on it (most publishers work largely on borrowed cash), and because they are aware that one of the factors which can tip the balance the wrong way between profit and loss is unearned advances (those which turn out to be substantially larger than the sums actually earned in royalties and from sub-licences). The 65% of earnings mentioned above is in fact an average sort of figure between the two extremes.

The MTA also lays down rules about how and when the advance should be paid. Publishers don't usually pay an advance in one go – at least, not in advance of publication. They prefer to pay out as little as they can before the book starts earning, and you cannot blame them for that – very considerable sums of money have to be invested before a book begins to bring in any income, and, as in any well-run business, one of the rules for success is to keep unnecessary costs down, including that of borrowing money. Most authors, on the other hand, would like to have any money going as soon as possible.

Advances are split in many different ways – part may be paid on signature of the agreement, or on delivery of the typescript, or on publication, or six months after publication, or on some other arbitrary date, and there are also many variations in the proportion of the total advance paid at different times. The MTA suggests two standard arrangements: if the book has not been commissioned, half the advance should be paid on signature of the contract and half within one year thereafter or on publication, whichever is the sooner (this gives the publisher an additional reason for not delaying publication); if the book is commissioned, one third of the advance should be paid on signature, one third on delivery of a final typescript (after revision, if necessary) and one third within twelve months of delivery or on publication, whichever is the sooner.

Royalties

Royalties are normally expressed as a percentage of the retail price of the book, with many different rates being paid according to the type of sale, the most notable difference being between the royalty paid on what are known as 'home sales' (usually sales within the British Isles) and that paid on export sales. Although different standards are used in most cases for children's books, educational and academic books, and for exceptional publications such as encyclopaedias and other compilations, packaged books, etc., most publishers accept the idea that the basic royalty on home sales for a hardcover book is 10% and on a paperback 7½%, and it is also been normal practice to increase these percentages after a certain level of sales has been achieved. Too often, however, the point at which the 10% royalty would increase to 12½% has been a totally unrealistic one from the author's point of view (rather like those vanity publishers who promise gullible authors that they will pay a huge royalty on all sales after the first 400, and then print 400 copies only, so that the target is never reached). The MTA says very firmly that the home royalty on hardcover editions of general books should go up to 12½% after 2500 copies, and to 15% after a further 2500 copies, have been sold.

Some publishers nowadays are moving away from the idea of paying royalties on the published price of the book, and calculate the royalty instead on the price they receive. This has the twin advantages for them of simplifying the whole calculation, especially since it is so easy to work out on the computer, and of making it unnecessary to include any special arrangements for exceptionally high discounts on sales. Naturally, the royalty rates are increased (typically starting at 16%) to ensure that the author does not lose by the arrangement.

The royalties on export sales are often expressed in publishers' agreements at half the rate for home sales. This may be fair in some cases when the cost of sales, including not only discounts but freight, is particularly high, but the MTA prefers the royalties to be based on the price received by the publisher, and asks for 10% of the receipts on the first 2500 copies sold, 12½% of receipts on the next 2500, and 15% thereafter.

You should also be prepared for the possibility that there will be no mention of either home or export sales in your contract, but that the varying royalty rates will be based on the different discounts which the publisher gives, regardless of where the books are sold. This is because it is no longer true that all sales in the home market are made at discounts substantially lower than those given to overseas customers, as was standard procedure in the past.

It should be pointed out that the royalty rates for children's books are commonly lower than those quoted above, primarily because of the additional costs of the illustrations and the need to keep the retail price at a low level (the public, which has a great many odd ideas about books, always expects children's books to be much cheaper than those for adults).

Different scales of royalties apply to a paperback produced by the publisher with whom the original contract is made. The MTA suggests a royalty of 7½% on the first 50 000 sales and thereafter 10% in the home market, and 6% on all copies sold for export. Again the rate for children's books is lower.

Paperback rights

If the publisher sub-licenses paperback rights to an outside concern, the moneys resulting from the deal will be split between publisher and author. In the past, publishers took 50% of all such income, but a fairer share for the author would start at 60% and rise later to 70%.

Bookclub sales

Bookclub deals are of two main kinds. The bookclub may purchase copies of the publisher's edition at a royalty-inclusive rate, in which case the author should receive 10% of the publisher's total receipts, or it may either manufacture the book itself or buy copies from the publisher at a non-royalty-inclusive rate, in which case it will pay royalties separately, and these should be divided between publisher and author so that the latter receives not less than 60%.

US rights, translation rights, subsidiary rights

The first point to note is that the author is not obliged to give the publisher US or translation rights or any subsidiary rights at all. Agents normally retain quite a number of rights, which they then attempt to sell on the author's behalf. If you do not have an agent, the publisher will undoubtedly wish to control all the rights, and it may be a very wise thing to allow him or her to handle them on your behalf, since the publishing house almost certainly employs an expert in these fields who will make considerable efforts to achieve good sales.

The MTA proposes the following percentages as the author's share of the publisher's receipts: US rights – 85%, or if the publisher sells sheets or copies of the British edition, usually with changes to the cover, title page, etc., at a royalty-inclusive rate (usually at a knock-down price), 10% to 15%; translation rights: 80%; second serial rights, condensation rights for magazines, strip cartoon rights, TV radio and recorded readings, one shot periodical: all 75%; condensation rights for books, and hardcover reprint, loose leaf and large print: all 50%; merchandising (a right which has vastly increased in importance in the last few years): 80%.

The rights listed above are those which most publishers will expect to control in most books. As already mentioned, agents normally retain some of them on the author's behalf, including especially US and translation rights, and also some which have not yet been listed. The latter include first serial rights, television and radio dramatisation, and film and dramatic rights. If you do allow the publisher to control and sell any of these rights on your behalf, your share of the proceeds should be not less than 90%, although you may have a struggle to get agreement to that figure.

One further case where the MTA proposes that the author should receive 90% of any proceeds is that of sub-licensed electronic or multimedia rights. The electronic exploitation of books and other written material is so new, so little understood, and so important a development, which is likely to change the face of publishing within a few years from now, that an entire chapter of this book is devoted to it (see Chapter 9).

Format, print quantity and retail price

Standard publishing agreements have rarely included any mention of the format. The MTA requires a publisher to state how the book will appear – in hardcover, paperback, or in some other special format. Additionally, the publisher is asked to include in the contract a statement of how many copies will be printed initially, and the proposed retail price of the book. These specifications cannot be binding on the publisher, because circumstances change so rapidly and significantly. The format originally planned may later seem not to be the best for the book, the print quantity originally envisaged may leap up or down dramatically according to the reception which the trade gives to early promotion by the publisher's sales force and by other means, and according to whether some outside event affects the expected sale, and of course the retail price may have to be altered in accordance with the final production costs, which can change substantially over quite a short period. However, the importance of the MTA clause is that it is another example of the principle of consultation.

Editorial alterations

The MTA specifies that the publisher shall inform the author of a commissioned book within thirty days of receipt of the completed typescript if any alterations to it are needed, and it then gives the publisher a further thirty days in which to specify exactly what the required changes are. Equally, if the publisher does not want to accept the book, the rejection must be notified to the author within thirty days after delivery, and detailed reasons for turning it down supplied within the following thirty days.

The author has the right to reject the publisher's demands for alterations, but if the latter is adamant that they are necessary, this may be tantamount to cancellation of the contract by the author, and that will mean returning any moneys already received, and a search to find a new publisher for the book. An author should not refuse to make alterations without very serious consideration. The first question that must be asked is whether the publisher might by any chance be right. On the whole, publishers don't ask for changes to be made simply for the sake of change. They are aiming to improve the quality of the book or its sales potential or both. Unless the alterations would offend the author's integrity or would change the whole book in a radical and unacceptable way, the suggestions should be adopted, or at least discussed with an open mind. Discussion should not only clarify the publisher's requirements, but may allow of compromise on certain points and even agreement in other cases that the text may remain unaltered.

Incidentally, in the world of television, if a writer is asked to do a substantial amount of rewriting, it is usual to be able to negotiate an additional fee for this work. That does not apply in the world of books, and publishers will expect authors to rewrite a whole book, if necessary, without any alteration in the terms of the contract and without any one-off payment for the additional work. They will argue, firstly, that the rewrite is necessary because the author did not turn in a fully competent work, secondly, that if the author refuses to do the work, the alternative exists of repaying any moneys already received for the book and trying to sell it elsewhere, and finally, that whatever the terms of the contract, the publisher has in the end the right to decide whether to publish or not.

I should make it plain that the editorial alterations referred to above are the changes, usually of a fairly important, structural nature, which the publisher wishes the author to make before accepting the book. They are not the detailed amendments of the typescript made or suggested by a copy-editor or line-editor before it goes to press, which we shall come to later in this chapter.

Copyright fees

Many authors feel that the cost of illustrations should always be borne by the publisher. Few publishers will agree, but it depends to some extent on circumstances, and whether it is the publisher's idea to include illustrations or the author's, and just how necessary they are. The MTA states bluntly that the publishers will pay for copyright fees for illustrations, or will at least contribute up to £250 towards the cost. As for copyright textual material, this is left for negotiation. Again, many authors will find that their publishers are not exactly enthusiastic about paying such fees.

Index

Books which require an index immediately pose a problem. Indexing is very much a specialist job, and few authors are really competent at it. The Society of Indexers can provide the necessary expertise, but at a cost which, while it is entirely justifiable given the meticulous attention to detail and knowledge of the craft required, can make a very substantial hole in an author's earnings. Publishers used to be quite unsympathetic on this score, and if the author was not competent to produce a reasonable index would expect him or her to pay for one that was. The MTA proposes that the cost in such cases should be shared between publisher and author.

The licence

The proposal to limit the licence period has already been discussed (see pp. 70-1), as has the fact that publishers are mostly opposed to any shortening of the traditional length of licence for the full period of copyright.

Happily, one of the other provisions of the licence clause in the MTA is currently proving rather more acceptable to many publishers, and that is the author's right to be fully informed of any sub-licences negotiated by the publisher, and indeed to be consulted about them before the deals are signed and sealed. As with any of the other matters in which the MTA suggests that consultation with the author should take place, while the publisher is honour-bound to give serious consideration to the author's views, little weight is likely to be placed on them unless the author is in the bestseller class and therefore has a great deal of power. So, if you think that a deal for a particular subsidiary right is not a good one, perhaps because you think the publisher is selling too cheaply, the publisher might agree to go back and ask for more, but is more likely to explain to you that you're lucky to get any deal at all, and that if the potential sub-licensee is pressed for more cash the whole deal may be abandoned, and that in any case that you don't understand the market. But, you may say, supposing the publisher owns a paperback house and proposes to sub-lease the paperback rights to the firm's daughter company, isn't it possible that a deal will be arranged which will let the subsidiary company buy the rights at a knock- down price? Yes, it is possible, but publishers are well aware that they have to justify giving their own subsidiaries first offer, or perhaps topping rights (the right to improve on any offer received from a competitor), and they will make sure that the price paid is a good one. If you have good reason to suspect that this is not the case, you would be justified in asking that the rights should be offered elsewhere before the deal is completed.

Reprographic rights

The MTA includes under the heading of 'Subsidiary Rights' a statement to the effect that reprographic rights shall be granted by the Author and the Publisher to the ALCS (Authors' Licensing and Collecting Society) and the PLS (Publishers' Licensing Society) respectively. Reprographic rights are those involved when your work is photocopied, and, as explained in Chapter 4, the CLA (Copyright Licensing Agency) collects fees for photocopying and passes 50% of them to the PLS and 50% to the ALCS for onward transmission to the publishers and authors concerned. The MTA clause goes on to say that any moneys due in respect of reprographic rights not controlled by the CLA shall be divided 50/50 between the author and the publisher.

Most publishers accept this arrangement without question, but in some cases, particularly with academic publishers, the author may have difficulty in getting the 50% share. You should not give in on this point if you can possibly avoid it, and certainly not without a fight.

Rights not covered in the agreement

It is most important to ensure that somewhere in the agreement is a clause or sub-clause stating that all rights not specifically mentioned in the contract are reserved by the author. This is essential because technical developments come so quickly nowadays that within a few years a whole string of new ways of exploiting a literary work may have been invented. Unless there is a clause in the contract specifically reserving any previously unknown rights to the author, the publisher will tend to feel that it is in order for him or her to sell any such rights. As I seem to keep on saying, most publishers are not unscrupulous cheats, and if such a case arose, would undoubtedly give the author a share in any return from it as a matter of course; nevertheless, the publisher's instinctive reaction when faced with any right not already covered in the agreement is that a fair share would be 50%. Well, it might be, but it also might not. Some negotiation would be necessary (for which the agentless author should take advice from the Society of Authors or the Writers' Guild or, at the least, from some knowledgeable fellow writer).

Return of the typescript

Once a book is published the publisher normally has no use for the typescript. It may be kept for a short while, in case any queries should arise, but will probably be consigned to the rubbish dump sooner or later – unless the author asks for its return, which is a right included in the MTA. Although one may never look at them again, typescripts are somehow rather nice to have – a great many of my author friends would agree with that – so, if for no other reason, it is worth asking for their return. But there is another possible justification, and this is that various institutions in the United States, mostly university libraries, are willing to pay good dollars for typescripts of published books. You do need to have a modest degree of fame, though you don't have to be a bestseller.

If you have supplied computer discs to your publisher (a practice which is rapidly becoming the norm), these too should be returned to you. I don't know whether any mad American would want to buy them, but even if they don't and even if you don't want to keep them for sentimental reasons (they don't have the same attraction as the neat pile of a well-produced typescript), you could of course always use them again for a new book.

Consultation

The MTA, while recognising the publisher's right to make the final decisions, demands that the author should be consulted over a number of matters, and in some cases should have the right of approval of the proposals (such approval not to be unreasonably withheld or delayed). Let us now look at specific matters under this general heading.

Copy-editing All sensible authors are grateful for the services of a good copy-editor, whose job is to prepare the typescript for the printer. The work extends far beyond merely correcting the author's slipshod grammar and spelling and punctuation, and often includes checking facts, eliminating inconsistencies, ambiguities and infelicitous phrasings, and generally polishing the author's work so that it is a good deal better than when it left the author's hands, and yet is not changed in any way which would distress the author by being untrue to his or her intentions or carefully considered style, or indeed to the whole spirit of the book. And in fact there are very few authors whose work cannot be improved in this way. A poor copy-editor, on the other hand, can make unnecessary and insensitive changes, rewriting the typescript in accordance with his or her own ideas, and imposing a straitjacket on the prose so that it loses its individuality.

(In some publishing firms the functions listed above are split, the copy-editor being responsible only for grammatical and typing errors, while a line-editor deals with the remaining matters. In other publishing houses, alas, copy-editors have disappeared, and the author's typescript goes to the printer without any cosmetic treatment.)

It is only right and proper that the author should be consulted about copy-editing changes, and, as the MTA proposes, should be given the right of approval of them, but, as in all matters of consultation, it is essential that the copy-editor's suggested changes should be discussed calmly and reasonably. If you really feel unable to accept the proposed alterations and the copy-editor insists that they should be made, you may find it worth appealing to higher authority within the publishing firm.

Changes in the title or the text   No such changes, says the MTA, should be made without the author's consent, or, it is to be hoped in all cases, without a full explanation from the publisher of why the change is thought to be necessary. The author's right to approve copy-editing is important enough. The right to approve a title or text change is equally so.

Illustrations   The MTA also states that the author should be consulted and has the right of approval over the final number and type of illustrations. This seems to me a fairly generous concession on the part of those publishers who have signed an MTA containing such a clause. Consultation is fair, but many publishers would look askance at a contract which allowed the author (as this clause seems to do) to turn the publisher's proposals upside down by demanding the inclusion of a larger number of illustrations than the publisher first intends. As for approval of the type of illustration, this might be all very well if the author had the right of veto over proposed illustrations which were inappropriate in some way, but again it sounds as though the author could be able to insist, for instance, that the pictures should be in full colour rather than in monochrome. The publisher does, of course, have the all-purpose escape wording that the author must not unreasonably withhold approval, but an awkward situation could develop.

It should be noted that illustrations in children's books often come into a very different category from those accompanying a non-fiction text for adults – they may be more important than the text, and even if that is not the case, will almost certainly be an essential part of the book, without which it would have little chance of success in its market. The MTA, as already explained, does not apply to books in which illustrations form 40% or more of the material (in which case, unless the author is responsible for both the text and the pictures, there will probably be separate agreements for author and artist), but all writers of books for children should be entitled, in my view, to full and serious consultation concerning the illustrations for their texts.

Publication date Here the MTA offers consultation, although I have to say that unless the author could put forward very convincing reasons, it would be very difficult to change the publisher's proposed date. However, consultation does at least mean that the author will know in advance when the book will appear, which has certainly not always been true in the past when publishers habitually took a more cavalier attitude towards their authors.

The jacket or cover design Almost all published authors have at some time in their writing career been dissatisfied, and indeed, occasionally greatly distressed, to find their books appearing in a jacket which seemed to be irrelevant, ugly, illegible or totally inappropriate for the book – or any combination of some or all of those faults. Happily, as already explained, consultation is now much more widespread than it used to be, and any sensible publisher will listen with respect to what the author has to say. Let me repeat that critical comments should be confined to facts – at least, if there is to be any hope that your views will result in a change. Adverse comments on the general effect of the jacket or cover are to be avoided or expressed extremely gently, because you will not be commenting on a matter of fact, but casting an aspersion on the artistic and possibly commercial taste of the publisher and the art director, and on their publishing expertise, and on the professional skill of the artist.

The blurb Authors should always be allowed to see the blurbs for their books, if only to correct any mistakes in the content or to protest if the blurb does not truly represent the book, but once again criticism is best confined to any matters of fact.

Publicity and promotion The Society of Authors has conducted a number of surveys to establish what their members think of their various publishers, and in a long list of questions about various aspects of publishing, the one on the subject of the publisher's performance in the area of publicity and promotion always gets a very poor reaction. No author is ever really satisfied with what the publisher does in this direction – and that is true even of bestselling authors. Don't imagine, if your publisher agrees to a clause in the contract which says that you will be consulted, that you will be able to exert much influence on the plans to promote and publicise (or not to promote and publicise) your book. Publishers tend to spend a lot of money on the big bestsellers on their lists, and not very much on the rest, and it is unlikely that you will be able to persuade them to change the allocations on which they have decided. Mind you, they will say, quite rightly, that as far as general books and fiction are concerned, the only effective way to publicise them is to spend a very large sum of money – medium- sized or small sums don't achieve anything, so there is little point in putting in a few extra hundred pounds. Neither do advertisements have much effect, they will tell you, unless the advertisements are huge and repeated and are part of a blanket-coverage campaign. If pressed, they will suggest that most publicity and promotion for books and their authors, other than bestsellers, is merely cosmetic, and achieves little except to keep the author from being too unhappy. This does not mean that they do nothing at all in this line. What publishers *will* do for your book is to advertise it in the trade press, get any free publicity they can, send out review copies, and, of course, do everything in their power to persuade booksellers to stock the book. Because that sort of thing is not generally visible to the public at large, the author may not think of it as publicity and promotion, but of course it is.

If all that is so, is there any point in the MTA's requirement that the publisher should ask the author for 'personal information relevant to publicity and marketing'? Well, yes, to the extent that the author may have access to a society or a mailing list of people who would be interested in the book, and may know, better than the publisher, of specialist journals in which an advertisement really would be worth while (and publishers are much more amenable to advertising in the specialist press than in national or provincial newspapers and magazines – after all, the smaller the journal, the less expensive the advertising costs will be).

The MTA also requires the publisher to ask the author for a list of people to whom review or free copies should be sent. Publishers will usually be willing to send out quite a large number of review copies – it is one of the cheapest forms of publicity available to them – and will do so especially to any reviewers who are really likely to publish a piece on the book because the author is known to them or is a local resident, or because they are particularly interested in the book's subject. The author's list of free copies (as opposed to those for review purposes) should not of course consist simply of the names of relatives and friends, but if the publisher can be convinced that the recipients of free copies will do something to promote the sales of the book, the books will usually be sent out.

The size of the first printing The MTA requires the publisher to inform the author of the number of copies which have been printed of the book. Such matters used to be closely guarded secrets – it was thought best to keep the publishing craft as a mystery (even Stanley Unwin's classic book, *The Truth About Publishing*, was written only in general terms), and many publishers are still reluctant to reveal such information, fearing that their authors will be disgruntled to find that the figures are lower than they expected, and will complain and perhaps take their next book elsewhere. Authors are not always the most realistic of creatures, and often find it difficult to accept the facts of publishing life. However, the main point is to further the relationship between publisher and author – if they really are partners, then there should be no secrets between them.

Publishers' agreements are negotiable

As a final point in this chapter, authors should remember that almost everything in a publisher's agreement is negotiable. You have a right not to sign an agreement without asking for a change in any of its clauses which seem to you less than satisfactory, or even unfair. The publisher may or may not agree to alter whatever it is that you are complaining about, but there's nothing to stop your asking, and the publisher, although perhaps unwilling to meet your point or prepared to go only halfway towards it, should at least explain why. Similarly, you have a right to ask for the clarification of anything in the agreement which you don't understand.

Never be afraid to take up any points about the contract with the publisher. As long as you are polite and reasonable in your attitude, there's no need to fear that the promise to publish your book will be withdrawn (the publisher will already have spent far too much time and money on it to want to do that) or even that you will be branded in the publisher's eye as a Difficult Author.

9
Electronic rights

The new buzz words

Multimedia, CD-ROM, interactivity, network publishing, virtual reality – these are some of terms which in the past five years or so have suddenly become in vogue wherever publishers and professional authors are gathered together. They all refer to the latest technological developments, and one of the problems for anyone trying to find their way around in this new world is that practical application of the technology is so new that there is some uncertainty about the exact meaning of the various terms. What they have in common is that they require new rights – electronic rights.

Multimedia technology is already a familiar part of daily life. Video images can be sent over telephone lines, and we and the people we talk to on the phone can already see each other if we have the right equipment. All forms of communication are in the process of being transformed – shopping, banking, betting and a consultation with the doctor are possible without setting foot outside your home. Some teachers already have the use of innovative aids, such as the ability to present their pupils with visual demonstrations on screen, with multi-choice options, of what they are teaching.

Multimedia 'books' are on the market and growing in popularity. What this means for writers and publishers is that the written text is displayed on the screen, rather than on a page (generally running through a computer fitted with a compact disc). But the text is enhanced with the addition of still or moving images, movie film-clips, sound, animation and so on – to make what might be called an 'all-singing, all-dancing' experience. The text may no longer be read in sequential order, but called up at the press of a button, so that the reader can pick a personal route through the 'book'. Sometimes this may mean choosing what happens next in a story. It is all rather frightening in some ways – how can a novelist, for instance, control what the twenty-first century reader does to the novel?

And what about CD-ROM? Well, 'CD' stands for 'Compact Disc' – just like the CDs which provide you with music - and 'ROM' stands for Read Only Memory (which means that, at the present time, you can only look at or listen to the material stored on the disc). CD-ROMs carry the software that produces the multimedia material. Play the disc, which is quite small, on a CD-ROM player attached to your PC (somewhat similar, but not the same as the CD player you use for music), and there you are – the multimedia facilities are at your finger tips.

If all this is new to you, it won't be for long. You may be asking if this means the disappearance of the book as we know it, and whether we shall all have to equip ourselves with portable machines on which to play these discs. Those who are working in the field seem to think that the ordinary book will survive, at least for a few more decades. 'I do not believe for a moment that books will become redundant,' says Sandy McKenzie of Phillips Media, and Alan Buckingham of Dorling Kindersley (one of the publishers who have taken a leading position in this field) says, 'The book is evolving. Multimedia is an addition, not a replacement.' Another prediction is that by the end of this century – only a few years away as I write – 15% of all new children's books, 25% of legal works, 25% of reference books, and 10% of fiction will be produced in multimedia versions. If you are not only horrified by these developments, but find it difficult to believe that books will really disappear, just remember all the other changes that modern technology has brought and think how incredible television and fax machines and the compact disc itself, to give just three examples, would have seemed in 1900. And if you're worrying about the inconvenience of carrying a portable computer around with which to read these discs, it can be small and slim and light and less of a burden than a transistor radio (which itself would have seemed pretty incredible even as little as fifty years ago). For those of us who have been brought up with books, the prospect of their death may seem terrible; for our great-grandchildren the ordinary book, hardcover or paperback, may well seem as outdated as the penny-farthing bicycle.

Electronic rights

Electronic rights are not a single discrete entity. Just as you expect to negotiate different terms for hardback rights, paperback, talking books, animation, etc., so you would want to control whether your text is used in a multimedia product, or a hand-held book, or included in an on-line database. Each of these ways of displaying the text is referred to as being a different 'platform', in the same way that a paperback is a different 'platform' from a talking book. At the last count, as I write, there were nineteen different platforms or types of platform, and the situation is changing all the time.

You may find most of the previous paragraph fairly incomprehensible, but even if you do not understand the technology, it is important to accept the facts that electronic rights are, as of now, of vital importance to both authors and publishers, and that as the originators of the raw material which can be produced in electronic form, the author must guard against unfair exploitation.

Publishers want authors to grant them 'all electronic rights' so that they can respond to opportunities as they arise. But it isn't necessarily in the author's best interests to sign away a blanket clause allowing the publisher to deal in all platforms. In order to get total control some publishers are using bullying tactics, refusing to sign contracts which do not grant them all electronic rights, and moreover offering royalties which any good trades unionist would describe as 'derisory'. Don't give in to the bullying, or accept any terms without first taking expert advice. The authors' union, the Society of Authors, is eager to protect authors from the sharks of the multimedia world, and has drawn up a list of important rules for all authors, set down in the order of priority:

1   You are advised to retain all electronic rights. That is to say, you should not grant them to the publisher at all, and it would be very sensible to include a clause in the agreement mentioning particularly that you are not licensing them to the publisher along with any other subsidiary rights. This will ensure that you have total control of the rights.

2   However, you may grant the publisher first refusal on particular and specified electronic use with each use being subject to the author's consent and on terms to be agreed; failing which,

3   You could grant specified electronic rights to the publisher, subject to the following:

(a) If electronic publishing is to be carried out by the original publisher, the advance, royalties, electronic format, duration of electronic publishing and other terms must be agreed before production and release for publication, with the publisher meeting any additional cost of material such as music, visuals, etc. The terms of the advance and royalties would not be less than those that the author could expect in a contract for a work to be published in traditional book format.

(b) If the publisher wishes to sub-license any electronic rights, the terms for each licence (especially its duration) should be subject to the author's approval and the income should be divided in proportions of at least 80% / 20% in the author's favour (and 90% for the author would not be unreasonable).

(c) All enquiries received by the publisher for electronic rights should be referred to the author for due consultation and approval.

(d) Electronic rights should revert to the author if not exploited within an agreed period (probably no longer than two or three years).

(e) All rights under the contract should revert to the author in the normal way when the work is out of print, even if an electronic version is still available (e.g. in a database).

(f) The author's work should not be altered in any way (except in format) and the publisher should agree to include such a condition in the sub-licence. In other words, the publisher must protect the author's Moral Right of Integrity (and this is particularly important because of what can happen if the use of the material includes interactivity – offering the 'reader' a choice of how to move through the material).

(g) The licence term should be of limited duration, say three to five years after release, to enable authors to benefit from successful titles or to avoid being locked into an unsuccessful technology.

Do note that item 1 above is the most important rule of all, and adhere to it if you can. Retaining all your electronic rights will not deprive you of income - it will simply mean that when the time to exploit the rights arrives you will not be unfairly treated because their control is still in your own hands. However, because some publishers, as already mentioned, are refusing to let their authors retain these rights, items 2 and 3 may be more realistic.

Seeking advice

If you have read as far as this in this chapter, you will have realised that we are on the edge of a new age for authors and publishers. How the new technology will develop is anyone's guess, and it is already so complicated that you undoubtedly need expert advice. You may be lucky, if you have an agent, to find that he or she is really at home in this new world, but few agents can boast of that. The best advice of all is probably that which is available from the Society of Authors or the Writers' Guild or the ALCS. If you have received an offer for a book from a publisher, you are entitled to join the Society even before you have signed the agreement, and then its considerable expertise will be at your beck and call.

Electrocopying

One of the other major problems with which authors and the producers of electronic material will have to cope is the infringement of copyright. Of course, your material is copyright as soon as it is written or recorded, and it remains copyright if it is transformed into an electronic version. It will bear the usual copyright line, and probably the symbol ©. However, just as unlawful photocopying of printed material is currently rife and difficult to control, electrocopying is going to be just as common. It is comparatively simple to make an electrocopy (rather like recording a television programme on your video machine, or making a duplicate disc on your word processor).

One possibility is that the Copyright Licensing Agency, which has already achieved a great deal in regulating the photocopying business, will be able to exercise some control over the problem by issuing licences to allow electrocopying on payment of a fee. The author's share of the moneys collected will no doubt be handed, as for photocopying, to the Authors' Licensing and Collecting Society, for onward transmission to the author. But that will not prevent home copying. The one real hope is that protective devices can be built into electronic material so that the ease of electrocopying will be seriously inhibited. The EU is currently putting considerable funding into the development of protection systems, with the intention of producing an international standard practice in this field.

10
Magazines and newspapers

FBSR (First British Serial Rights)

The rights which you sell when a magazine or newspaper buys your work are not the same as those you sell to a book publisher. The latter expects to be given a licence covering volume rights (and usually various other rights too) and, unless he or she is taking world rights, will also append to the agreement a list of those countries in which the licence will apply. A magazine or newspaper, on the other hand, apart from an increasing number of rogue examples who will try to grab your copyright, will in most cases be content with serial rights in one particular area only.

The word 'serial' in this context does not necessarily have anything to do with the publication of a work in instalments. It is not your work, but the magazine or newspaper which publishes it, which is a 'serial' in this case, 'serial' being a noun, one definition of which is 'a periodical publication'. 'Serial' is also used in this sense in 'International Standard Serial Number' (ISSN), the magazine world's equivalent of International Standard Book Number (ISBN).

Serial rights come in several forms, and the first question to examine is whether they are first or second serial rights. 'First' in this context refers to the fact that the work has not been published previously. In the case of short stories or articles there is usually little confusion about the first use of serial rights, but the situation with books is, or seems to be, rather more complicated. When serial rights are sold in a book and it (or extracts from it) is published in a magazine or newspaper before the book has been published in volume form, the serial rights are 'first' serial rights. If the work is sold for publication in a magazine or newspaper after it has appeared in book form, then the rights concerned are 'second' serial rights, even if it hasn't been published in a magazine or newspaper previously. As if the word 'serial' were not confusing enough, 'second' does not necessarily mean that this is the only time that the serial rights have been sold after first publication - however many times the rights are sold, they are not referred to as 'third' or 'fifth' or 'umpteenth' serial rights, but always as 'second' serial rights.

The other variation in the form of serial rights comes about because they are almost invariably divided up by territory, according to the origin of the magazines or newspaper. So, if you begin by selling your work to a British magazine or newspaper, you will sell First British Serial Rights (or possibly, nowadays, First European Serial Rights, since the European Union is considered as being indivisible). Many Creative Writing tutors advise you to put the magic letters FBSR (which stand for First British Serial Rights) on the top sheet of submissions to newspapers and magazines – in fact, in the case of newspapers it is unnecessary to use the initials or write the words out in full, or, indeed, to make any mention of the matter at all; a newspaper will take it for granted that that is what it is getting. It is not advisable to try to sell the same material to another British magazine or newspaper until some time has elapsed after that first publication, but if you then succeed in doing so – you may even re-sell it more than once – you will be selling Second British Serial Rights.

The same system applies to other countries, so that, although you may have sold First and Second British Serial Rights, if you then sell the same material to a magazine or newspaper in the United States (or Australia or Other English-Speaking Country), you would be selling First US (or First Australian, or First Other English-Speaking Country) Serial Rights and you could then go on, if you were fortunate enough, to sell Second US (Australian or Other English-Speaking Country) Serial Rights in those territories. 'First', in this context, always means first in the country concerned. And, in just the same way, if you sell your work in a foreign language, you will sell First or Second Serial Rights in that language.

In all these cases, the purchase of serial rights allows a magazine or newspaper to publish the work once, and once only. The one exception to this rule is that of a newspaper which produces several editions, either on the same day, or perhaps for different parts of the region which it covers, when the different editions are counted as one use. Some magazines sometimes produce anthologies of articles which have appeared in their issues over a previous period of time; they are not entitled to include your work in such a book if you have sold them first or second serial rights only.

Copyright

The work that an author writes for publication in a magazine or newspaper is subject to exactly the same rules of copyright as those applying to a book. The copyright period and the protection are the same, with the one exception that Moral Rights are not attached to such pieces (see below).

Not many magazines are prepared to print a separate copyright notice for their contributors, and newspapers never do. You will find that most magazines carry a copyright notice in the name of the proprietor (usually somewhere near the publisher's name and address, the name of the editor and other such details), but this really refers to the layout and the typography of the magazine, the editorial input and to the material which has been written by members of the staff. A few periodicals will copyright each issue in the name of their proprietors and then add some such wording as 'and contributors respectively' (*The Author* is a magazine which does this, perhaps not surprisingly since it is the journal of the Society of Authors). Fortunately, the printing of a copyright notice is not an essential item in the protection of your copyright, and most magazines and newspapers recognise that any published work (unless it is obvious that the author died a very long time ago) is likely to be in copyright, whether the copyright is held by the author or by the magazine or newspaper.

Although for most of the time you do not need to worry unduly, an increasing number of unscrupulous editors will pinch your copyright material if they can. You should try never to give in to those who want you to assign copyright in your work to them, because if you do, the proprietors of that magazine can use your work, if they so wish, in all their other publications, sell it to publishers abroad, re-publish it in book form, and so on, without paying you a penny piece more. Apart from your own interests in the matter, a principle is involved and if you surrender your copyright you are letting down other authors. Write 'FBSR' on your work when you submit it, and argue against any attempt to make you sell anything other than that. Don't, however, imagine that putting those initials on your piece gives you total protection – the tougher magazine publishers are quite capable of ignoring it. But the 'FBSR' is there as an initial statement of what you are offering, and if you have put it on your work it does give you the opportunity of saying, when you refuse to sign away your copyright, 'You must have known that I was offering serial rights only.'

The publishers of academic and scientific journals almost always insist on the surrender of the author's copyright. Other magazines have taken comparatively recently to telling their contributors that unless they are willing to give the magazine full copyright they will never work for that magazine again. Unfortunately, those contributors need to eat, and so many of them are forced to give in to the blackmail. The National Union of Journalists and the Institute of Journalists campaign constantly and vigorously against this situation, and are of course supported by other authors' organisations, but the best hope seems to lie in the European Union, which in general accepts that authors should not be deprived of their copyright, and seeks to persuade the member states to harmonise their regulations in this respect.

Some magazines can be quite sneaky, waiting until they send a cheque in payment for your work before there is any mention of copyright. On the back of the cheque is a form of wording stating that the copyright in the work is assigned to them, and they expect you to sign this before you pay the cheque in to your bank. There is an implication that if you don't sign, the cheque will bounce. Don't believe that. Simply cross out the wording stamped on the back. The cheque will usually go through, but if the magazine's publisher does protest, again you have the choice of acceptance or possible loss of a future market.

Even worse are those magazines who say nothing at all about copyright to the unsuspecting author, who thinks all is well until the magazine comes out with a notice saying that the work is the copyright of the magazine. This can happen despite the fact that you have clearly marked FBSR on your typescript. What can you do? You can sue, but the costs will probably stop you from doing so. The moral is that you must always clarify the position – as well as putting FBSR on the typescript, write to the magazine when you have an acceptance from them and remind them that all you are offering is serial rights – *not* copyright.

Encyclopaedias and yearbooks hardly come under the heading of this chapter, but since contributors to them are usually the authors of articles rather than of book-length works, it may be justifiable to comment on the position which their publishers frequently adopt. This is, as has already been mentioned in the chapter on copyright, that they ask their contributing authors to surrender their copyright so that they can have complete control of the book as a whole. However, in most instances where reputable publishers are concerned, the author can at least expect that the publisher will pay an additional fee each time that the work is reprinted, and a further sum if he or she is required to rewrite the material in order to update it.

A further copyright problem which writers for magazines and newspapers can meet is the result of the wording of the 1988 Act in respect of the copyright in work written for an employer. Such work is the employer's copyright. However, during the drafting of the Bill, a powerful lobby of magazine publishers managed to delete a clause which would have restricted the publisher's use of the copyright to publication in one or more of the company's magazines or journals, leaving the writer with the freedom to use the work in other forms. Magazine publishers in Europe, seeing the success of their British counterparts, are trying to follow the same practice. It is to be hoped that the European Union's directives on copyright will solve this problem too.

A different and interesting aspect of copyright affects an author who interviews someone, recording what the interviewee says on tape, or in shorthand or longhand, with the intention of turning the interview into a feature article. As soon as the spoken word is recorded, it becomes copyright, and the copyright belongs to the speaker, even though the recording is done by someone else. So before using verbatim quotes, the interviewer should clarify the matter with the subject of the interview, getting permission, preferably in writing, to use the material.

Moral Rights

Because Moral Rights do not apply to work published in newspapers and magazines, you are not protected in the same way as with a book, and you are very much in the hands of the editor and the sub-editors. Since you have no Right of Paternity, it is possible that your name will not appear as the author of the piece you have written, especially if you are writing for a magazine which frequently includes items which are not attributed to an author. Most magazines, however, are prepared to acknowledge your authorship. Newspapers will normally give a byline to feature articles, but will probably not do so for freelance news items.

Where you are likely to suffer more than over your byline is with editing. In book publishing it is gradually becoming accepted that no changes should be made to an author's work without his or her approval. The Right of Integrity is intended to cover rather more drastic reworking than a book publisher's normal copy-editing, but it could be invoked if you felt that the copy-editor who worked on your book had gone too far and without consulting you. In the world of newspapers and magazines, the Right of Integrity does not exist, but the right of the sub-editor to cut and rewrite your material does. Your work can be substantially mutilated, and chunks are often cut out solely because there is too little space available. Most professional sub-editors do a good job, and some are expert at making silk purses out of sows' ears, but there are those who can hack away with little care and turn your carefully structured piece into an almost incoherent muddle. What can you do if that happens? Very little, although in a bad case you might certainly protest to the editor. You could also decide not to write for that magazine or newspaper again. Alternatively, you could cry all the way to the bank.

Contracts and letters of agreement

There is at least one considerable advantage to an author if a magazine offers a contract in respect of an accepted or commissioned piece – the author then knows where he or she stands. The contract is likely to include details of the rights which the magazine expects to be granted and of the financial terms, the two items which the author may consider to be the most important. Dangers also lie in such contracts, because it is here that you may find either an unequivocal statement that the magazine will own the copyright in the article or story, or a clause under which you would assign 'all rights', or perhaps 'world rights' to the magazine. ('All rights' is, incidentally, much the nastier of the two phrases, since it could be taken to include copyright, whereas 'world rights' would probably not.) There may also be less alarming clauses, which you may nevertheless not like very much, such as one which gives the magazine the right to re-publish your work in an anthology. So what do you do? You strike out anything in the contract about which you are unhappy, and write in alternative wording limiting what you are granting perhaps to First or Second Serial Rights only for the country concerned. Don't be afraid to do this. Authors do have rights, and publishers and editors will usually give in if faced with an author's firm, but always polite, request for a fair arrangement. If the magazine writes back to insist on your agreement to the terms they originally offered, then once again you have to make the decision whether to go ahead or not. It may be very difficult to turn down the opportunity of seeing your work in print, but stand on your principles if you can possibly persuade yourself to do so.

In fact, however, formal contracts are comparatively rare in this field, and you are more likely to have at most a fairly brief letter. Letters can be regarded as legal contracts, but they are often rather vague, and you need to be careful about accepting them as they stand. Since you will probably be writing a letter back to the magazine or newspaper, you can take the opportunity of amending any matters or covering any missing points. If you don't make any changes, the magazine or newspaper will be entitled to assume not only that you accept everything set out in their letter, but also that you will go along with their standard position in respect of questions which have not been specifically covered. So, if there is no mention of copyright, for instance, and you do nothing about it, you may find that the magazine will assume that you have granted them full copyright in your piece.

Payment of fees

The fees which magazines pay vary considerably, according to the size of their circulations and retail price. As for newspapers, the NUJ (National Union of Journalists) publishes an annual guide laying down the rates which it considers fair, and even if you are not an NUJ member, you can usually persuade a newspaper to pay you at that standard. The money that you will receive will, of course, be an outright payment. You may have heard or read that outright payments are absolutely anathema to most professional writers and to bodies like the Society of Authors. But don't be confused. Outright payments are an abomination only when they cover copyright, or all rights, or even any lesser definition of rights which allows the purchaser to exploit the work in a comparatively unlimited way. Outright payments for a one-time use – for the purchase of first or second serial rights – are standard practice and entirely acceptable, provided, of course, that the amount is a fair one.

Magazines and newspapers normally pay contributors on publication, or shortly thereafter, rather than in advance, and newspapers in particular often do not pay unless the author sends in an invoice once his or her piece has appeared in print. This places an unfair burden on the author, who has to keep buying the magazine or newspaper to see if the piece is in it, for although an author will sometimes be told that his or her work is going to appear in a certain issue, it is frequently the case that the article or story is accepted without any firm publication date being given. Even if the author is told that the work will be printed in such and such an issue, there may be an editorial change of mind about the date. As someone pointed out recently, the insistence on payment on publication rather than on acceptance is directly parallel to going into Marks & Spencer in April to get some winter woollies and saying, 'I shan't be wearing these until October, so I shan't pay for them till then.' It is all very unfair. Unfair or not, it is the way things work, and it applies whether your piece is accepted after you have submitted it on spec, or whether you were commissioned to write it.

Sometimes editors keep material which they have commissioned or accepted for months before publishing it. Sometimes they decide that they will not publish after all. If this happens, the author should be entitled to what is known as 'a kill fee', which is a proportion of what you would have been paid if the work had been published. Not all magazines and newspapers pay kill fees, and authors do not have any legal right to be paid for work which is not used unless they have been given a contract or a letter which sets out their rights unequivocally. Nevertheless, it is always worth asking for some payment – you ought to get at least 50% of the originally agreed fee, but may have to settle for less.

11
Plays, films, television, video, radio

Basic rights

Authors of dramatic scripts (including documentaries), whether for stage, cinema, television or video, and of radio broadcast material have most of the same rights as authors of books or articles. Their work is copyright on exactly the same basis and terms, and they have similar protection against plagiarism. If their work is published in volume form and is available in Public Libraries, they will qualify for Public Lending Right and their reprographic rights can be handled by the Copyright Licensing Agency.

A distinction must be made, however, between the script of a film, whether used in the cinema, on television or in video form, and the finished work. The author's copyright extends only to the script, while the film itself is usually the copyright of the producer, which is currently the norm in the United Kingdom, or of the director, which is the standard arrangement in most other countries in the European Union. However, a new directive (which member states must obey) from the European Council will allow the scriptwriter of a film to be named as a 'co-author', and therefore co-owner of the copyright.

While this directive is to the benefit of scriptwriters, it is worth remembering, on the other hand, that no effective legislation has been brought forward in the United Kingdom to protect the copyright in anything which is copied on video in the home, nor has Brussels yet produced any dictats on this subject.

Dramatists, authors of screenplays, and writers for television and radio also enjoy the same Moral Rights as authors of books. Again, it is necessary to assert the so-called Right of Paternity, and this should be done at the time of the signing of any agreement in respect of the work. As already stated elsewhere, however, you are very likely to find that you are expected to waive your Moral Rights, and that refusal to do so will mean that the contract is cancelled. This is very unfortunate, but at the present time it would seem that only the most prestigious, popular and therefore powerful of writers can hope to resist.

As with books, you should not surrender your copyright in any material that you write for stage, cinema, radio, television or video. If your work is accepted you will license only the appropriate rights (e.g. the dramatic rights for the stage), and you will be free to exploit your material in other media if you wish, or to license someone else to adapt it for a different use.

As has already been stated, ideas are not copyright, and many authors who target their writing at radio or television feel that they are at greater risk of having their ideas pinched than authors of books. It is certainly true that a television company could snaffle your idea for a new sitcom or soap, while rejecting your own script. However, it is equally possible that, although this appears to be the case, some other author or someone in the television company has dreamed up the same idea just ahead of you. As already mentioned elsewhere, in her book *Writing for Radio* Rosemary Horstmann refers to some 'evidence for a climate of ideas, which leads to several people thinking along the same lines simultaneously.' Perhaps it is naive of me, but I still cling to my belief that the professionals in radio and television are no more likely to steal your ideas than are book publishers. However, Ms Horstmann goes on to say that some lawsuits claiming plagiarism of ideas have been successfully brought, so perhaps it would be wise to take her advice and deposit a sealed copy of your material in a bank, or post it to yourself at the same time as you submit it to a radio or television company so as to establish when it was written, and of course you should keep any relevant correspondence.

Altering the script

Where scripts for radio, television, videos, films and plays differ from books is that a number of other creative artists are likely to be involved in bringing the works before the public, so that you might say that the book publisher's editor is likely to be replaced not only by a script editor, but also by the director, the producer and the actors involved. Just as the editor of a book should not alter anything without your approval, so your dramatic work should be faithfully reproduced – but, of course, with those other creative artists to please, it is to be expected that many changes will be made in the course of rehearsals. The author is entitled to attend at least some of the rehearsals, and is there not only as a right, but also so that he or she can be asked to rewrite this, or cut that or add something else, or to approve an alteration made by the director or an actor (or anyone else, for that matter). Any changes which are made in this way – that is to say, which are agreed by the author and accepted by the director – become the author's property and are fully protected by copyright. (Incidentally, it is never wise to discuss any amendments to your script with anyone other than the director. Although the author and the director are regarded as equal partners, in practice the director is boss, so if, for instance, an actor says that a certain line is virtually impossible to say with any clarity or is 'not what my character would say' and asks you to rewrite it, refer the matter to the director before agreeing even to consider it, let alone actually making a change.)

Terms

Any author who writes for stage, film, television, video or radio almost certainly needs an agent, and that applies even if you are involved only in the occasional short story or talk for BBC radio. You will not be surprised to learn that it is extremely difficult to find an agent who will take you on if you are unknown. However, it will prove much easier once you have had work accepted.

It would not be unreasonable to suppose that there would be comparatively few problems which require an agent's intervention when dealing with the BBC, since the Corporation has a standard scale of fees and standard contracts. The fees, negotiated regularly with the Society of Authors and the Writers' Guild, are based on the length of transmission, and differ according to a number of points, such as whether the work is an original play, or a series or a serial, whether the writer has provided the storyline as well as the script or is working on a storyline which was provided, or whether the author is 'established' or a beginner. Similar arrangements apply to ITV contracts.

In the case of radio, the BBC terms are laid down in the same way, and again there is a wide range of payments, depending on such factors as whether the material is for general broadcasting or for schools, whether it is used on one of the 'home' services or on the World Service, whether the author is 'established' or a beginner, and of course there are different rates for features, plays, talks, etc.. Local radio, if controlled by the BBC, will use its formulae, but independent radio stations are likely to negotiate each case separately.

For both radio and television, provision is made for payments for 'repeat' use.

Details of all the fees can be obtained from the people who pay them, or from the Society of Authors or the Writers' Guild if you are a member. Even for a beginner, the sums involved are not ungenerous. So why is an agent necessary? Principally to ensure that your other rights are covered or reserved. The BBC is generally fair, but needs to save money if possible, so it is not above exploiting an author's ignorance by, for instance, offering an All Radio Rights contract, which would give the BBC the right to re-broadcast your material for an unlimited number of times without making any further payment - and you should certainly not accept that.

You may also be disappointed to discover that local radio stations are entirely unwilling to pay a fee if you appear on a chat-show to talk about your newly-published book, or your new play, or other work; they contend that they're giving you free publicity, and although you can argue, you probably won't get anywhere.

Once you start considering the sale of dramatic scripts to any of the media covered in this chapter, the need for professional advice becomes clear, since there are so many aspects of the agreement that you are likely to be offered which could be of crucial importance. Starting at the beginning, these include, for a stage play, options for both British and US production. Some clarification of the word 'options' is perhaps needed. In the world of book publishing, options normally refer to the author's next work or works, and both the Society of Authors and the Writers' Guild (supported by many literary agents) advise strongly against signing an option clause. The situation is, however, rather different for plays or films, for in those spheres the taking of options is to be welcomed. It is quite usual for the company which hopes to produce a play to take an option on it, with a payment to the author, in order to give itself time to raise the substantial sums which are necessary for a new stage production, to find the stars, and generally to make sure that the whole proposition is viable before going ahead. The same sort of thing applies to an option taken on material which may eventually be used as the basis for a film.

The agreement will also cover the licence period, which not only restricts the period for which the management has exclusive rights to the play, but ensures that the play will be produced within a specified time after signature of the contract. Further clauses cover various rights in which the management and the author will share, such as repertory rights and amateur rights, as well as radio, television, video and film rights. The agreement will of course also specify the moneys to be paid to the playwright, including the 'consideration' (a non-returnable one-off payment when the contract is signed), the advance against royalties (usually known as 'the acceptance fee'), the royalties on box office receipts, and perhaps a fee and expenses for the author's attendance at rehearsals. Also of importance are the clauses covering the author's right to approve the casting (and sometimes the set design), the fact that any alterations to the script can be made only with the author's approval and are his or her copyright, the credits to the author which will appear in publicity for the play and on the programmes, and the arrangements for granting the author free tickets to the performances. And of course there must be adequate clauses covering the rendering of accounts, arrangements for sub-leasing of the rights granted, and the conditions for termination.

Similar details have to be ironed out in contracts for films and television – in the latter case, there must be adequate provision for the payment of repeat fees if the material is re-broadcast. It really is a minefield for an inexperienced author, and a further indication of the complexities of the business is the fact that many literary agents do not deal with any kind of performing rights, and will pass your work to specialists in the field. If you don't want to have an agent, or can't get one, then you should at least join the Writers' Guild (which has particular expertise in screenwriting) or the Society of Authors.

Foreign rights

For a play which is to be translated and performed in a foreign country (or in English in the United States), a separate agreement will probably be drawn up, either directly with the playwright or with the management if the latter has been granted a licence for world rights. Scripts for films and television, on the other hand, are usually bought under contracts which give the original producers the right to have the film or television show shown throughout the world, either in the original, or with sub-titles or in a dubbed version. There should be adequate provision for payment to be made to the author in respect of any such sales, but very often in the case of films it will come under the general percentage of profits which the author enjoys. (Incidentally, it is always preferable to take a small percentage on gross profits than a large percentage on net profits.) So the film or television company will pay for exploitations of the material.

One exception to that rule is with the use of cable or satellite to transmit television programmes in foreign countries, when it is frequently the responsibility of the foreign company which takes such programmes to pay the scriptwriters their due fees. These moneys are usually sent to ALCS (see page 43), which then distributes them to the authors concerned.

Index

National Union of Journalists,
113-14, 117
newspapers, 18, 35, 111-18

obscene libel, 4, 11-13, 70
offensive material, 4-16, 69-70
options, 81-2, 122
out of print, 46, 50, 91-2, 109
outright payments, 23, 117

packaged books, 95
paperbacks, 40, 52, 60, 93, 95, 96, 97
   rights, 25, 77, 78, 96, 100
passing off, 32
Paternity, Right of 33-5, 86, 112-13,
   115-16, 119
permissions, 50-6, 69, 115
   acknowledgements, 55-6
   fees, 54-5
photocopying, 45-9, 59, 100
   licences, 47-8
photographs, 33, 53, 55
piracy, 24, 28-9
plagiarism, 4-8, 26-7, 69-70, 119, 120
plays, 119-23
PLR, see Public Lending Right
PLS, see Publishers Licensing
   Society
political correctness, 4, 14-16
pornography, 4, 11-13
press releases, 33
print, out of, 46, 50, 91-2, 109
print quantity, 72-3, 93, 97, 105
promotion, 71, 91, 97, 103-5
proofs, 86-7
pseudonyms, 32-3
Public Lending Right, 36-44, 89-90,
   119
public libraries, 36-44, 45, 47, 119
publication, 1-4, 62-105, 117-118
   date, 25, 72, 73-4, 83-4, 103,
      117-18
   delays, 74, 84, 91
publicity, 65, 71, 73, 80, 103-5, 122
publisher's rights, 62-82
Publishers Association, 29, 51, 63
Publishers Licensing Society, 47,
   48, 100

quotation rights, 60, 77

radio, 119-23
   rights, 96, 97
reference books, 35, 39, 64, 77
rejection, 2, 3, 26, 27, 82, 98
remainders, 79-81, 90, 91
reprints, 75-6, 92
reprographic rights, 45-9, 100, 119
retail price, 72, 93, 97
returns, 78-9
reversion of rights, 70, 83, 90-2, 109
review copies, 71, 104-5
revised editions, 40, 76-7
rights, author's, 83-105
rights, grant of, 66
royalties, 64, 79, 80, 85, 87, 88-9, 90,
   93, 94-6, 108, 122
royalty
   periods, 79, 88-9
   statements, 58, 87, 88, 89, 90

satellite television, 43, 123
scientific journals, 113-14
sedition, 4, 14
self-publishing, 3, 39, 40, 69
serial rights, 24, 60, 77, 96, 97,
   111-15
Society of Authors, *passim*
speeches, copyright in, 18
stage plays, 119-23
sub-licences, 33, 77-8, 89, 91, 94,
   96-7, 99-100, 109
subsidiary rights, 24, 60, 65, 77-8,
   96-7, 100-1, 106-10, 122
   anthology, 60, 77
   bookclub, 25, 60, 77, 96
   condensation, 96
   dramatic, 97
   electronic, 97, 106-10
   film, 97
   foreign language, 25, 57, 59, 77,
      96-7, 112, 123
   large print, 40, 97
   loose leaf, 96-7
   merchandising, 97
   one-shot periodical, 96
   paperback, 25, 60, 77 , 78, 96, 100